Being a Pastor:

a conversation with Andrew Fuller

Andrew Fuller's pulpit

Being a Pastor:

a conversation with Andrew Fuller

Michael A.G. Haykin & Brian Croft

with Ian H. Clary

EP BOOKS (Evangelical Press)

Registered Office: 140 Coniscliffe Road, Darlington, Co Durham, UK DL3 7RT

www.epbooks.org
admin@epbooks.org

EP Books are distributed in the USA by:
JPL Books, 3883 Linden Ave. S.E.,
Wyoming, MI 49548

www.jplbooks.com
orders@jplbooks.com

First published 2019

British Library Cataloguing in Publication Data available

ISBN 978-1-78397-274-6

What a rich and helpful work this is! Here is a book more than worthy of the attention of all who serve in pastoral ministry today, the world over. Not only does it contain ordination sermons and related materials on the ministry by the too often neglected but truly worthy 18th-century giant Andrew Fuller but it also takes opportunity to call on fellow ministers to avoid being lured away by popular but all too often empty and unbiblical modern strategies. We are called rather to mine the riches of the past, so attractively presented in this volume.

We must look first to Scripture but we are encouraged also to make good use of the best examples from the past, examples such as that of Fuller, who in his day preached and took such a radically biblical approach to pastoral leadership. The book teems with helpful insights into pastoral ministry and by God's grace will help pastors to understand their calling, strive for usefulness, cultivate their affections, pursue faithfulness and focus always on Christ—the very things we so need in these testing times.

Gary Brady, Pastor, Childs Hill Baptist Church, London

Pastoral ministry has always been a privilege and a responsibility for those called to that office. This relatively short book of nineteen ordination sermons by a master practitioner of a former era provides very helpful guidance not only to those starting out in ministry, but equally serves as a refresher course to others with many years of service. These sermons provide easily applicable principles for Christian ministry in the twenty-first century and are encouraging but also deeply challenging as we reflect on church practice today. This book is warmly commended.

Brian Talbot, Minister of Broughty Ferry Baptist Church, Dundee,
& Professor in the Dept of Theology, North-West University, South Africa

Some books on pastoral ministry press upon the heart with practical, spiritual directions. Some books shine a light into dark, neglected attics to reveal forgotten treasures of our historical heritage. This book does both, and I heartily commend it to your reading.

Joel R. Beeke, President, Puritan Reformed Theological Seminary, Grand Rapids, Michigan

How refreshing it has been to sit at the feet of Andrew Fuller and drink in words of deep piety, practical wisdom, and rare balance. We should read these sermons on our knees. It is my prayer that this volume will be mightily used to reorient and refocus our present generation of Christian ministers.

Carl Muller, Pastor, Trinity Baptist Church, Burlington, Ontario

Both the rich spiritual ministry of Andrew Fuller, exemplified here in ordination sermons he preached and the wise pastoral counsel contained in this volume will serve you well. If you are a young man considering pastoral ministry you will find much helpful instruction in this volume. If you are a more seasoned pastor it will renew and refresh your soul in your service of your King.

Elderships, local pastoral gatherings and any form of pastoral training whether in the local church or seminary class would do well to work through this volume. It will be an exercise rich in spiritual encouragement and comprehensive in biblical instruction regarding the greatest work in all the world. It informs the mind, stirs the affections and directs the will with clarity and warmth.

Robert Briggs, Pastor, Immanuel Baptist Church, Sacramento, California
& President of Reformed Baptist Seminary, Sacramento, California

Here is a treasure trove of good, biblical advice on pastoral ministry, found in ordination sermons preached by the Baptist pastor and theologian, Andrew Fuller. These are helpfully set in context by chapters on eighteenth-century ordination sermons in Dissent more generally and on Andrew Fuller's view of pastoral ministry in particular. We have much in common with these men. These were not the itinerant preachers of the revivals, who often had no local body of believers to care for; they received no support from the state and suffered social and economic disadvantages for their principled decision to dissent from the establishment; and they did not enjoy the status and public esteem which many of their nineteenth-century successors would do. They were men devoted to local church ministry, pastoring a flock, often with little in the way of numerical encouragement and battling many of the same challenges that evangelical pastors do today. There is a great deal that we can learn from these sermons, expertly brought together with helpful commentary by the compilers and editors. The closing section, applying Fuller's principles to pastoral ministry today, is challenging, clear, and of the utmost relevance.

Robert Strivens, Pastor, Bradford on Avon Baptist Church, Bradford on Avon, Wiltshire

Among the great Baptist pastor-theologians, none stands as pre-eminently pastoral as Andrew Fuller. Through his sermons, treatises, and other works, Fuller sought to pastorally instruct his people in the rigours of theological and biblical understanding. This timely book is a clarion call to successive generations to emulate Fuller's example of what it truly means to be a pastor-theologian.

Steven J. Lawson, President, OnePassion Ministries, Dallas, Texas

With so many pressures on the modern pastor, this historical exposition of pastoral ministry is a breath of fresh air. These ordination sermons emphasise the priority of preaching, devotion to Christ, godliness, and love for people, but also include a treasury of practical wisdom. Fuller's own spiritual devotion and earnestness shine through as a model for us.

Bill James, Principal, London Seminary

Thoroughly biblical, historical and practically helpful, this book presents us with a clear call as pastors to keep a watch over ourselves and over the flock God has entrusted to our care. The ordination sermons by Fuller were a joy to read and a trove of pastoral wisdom and insight. The analysis in the closing chapters distill the pastoral theology of the book, anchoring everything in scripture. This book will be a great blessing to pastors and would be a great addition to any pastoral theology syllabus!

Steve Auld, Pastor, Great Victoria Street Baptist Church, Belfast

One of the striking things about reading the lives and writings of pastors from the past is how contemporary the challenges of pastoral ministry from previous centuries seem. There is the perennial need for doctrinal fidelity, personal piety, perseverance through difficulties, and, above all, reliance upon the Holy Spirit. Andrew Fuller's ordination sermons reflect the wisdom of the ages distilled at a particularly remarkable era in the history of the church by one of its most noteworthy servant-leaders. I am thrilled to see this wisdom made available to a new generation of ministers who need to face the age-old challenges with the same graces of the Spirit.

Steve Weaver, Pastor, Farmdale Baptist Church, Frankfort, Kentucky

The eighteenth-century Baptist pastor Andrew Fuller has a lot to teach us today about the privilege and the shape of gospel ministry. Reformed and outward-looking, Fuller shared his vision for a godly and evangelistic ministry in his letters and sermons to ordinands, which are helpfully reproduced, expertly contextualised, and warmly applied in this useful volume by Michael Haykin, Brian Croft, and Ian Clary. There is much here to stimulate, challenge, and inspire ordinands and ministers today, whatever their denominational background.

Lee Gatiss, Director of Church Society & Lecturer in Church History, Union School of Theology

Andrew Fuller's ordination sermons have been, outside of the Bible itself, my most important reading for pastoral nourishment. Fuller's persistent call for the pastor to pursue the truth as it is in Jesus and to approach all of his ministerial tasks first as a Christian, then as a minister, has reoriented my thinking toward the gospel countless times when I have been drifting toward an unfeeling, self-referential, and merely transactional approach to ministry. With trusted guides like Michael A.G. Haykin, Brian Croft, and Ian Clary, I cannot commend this volume heartily enough.

David E. Prince, Pastor of Ashland Avenue Baptist Church, Lexington, Kentucky & Assistant Professor of Christian Preaching, The Southern Baptist Theological Seminary

As it is said of Abel that "through his faith, though he died, he still speaks" (Hebrews 11:4), the eighteenth-century Baptist pastor, Andrew Fuller, speaks to the nature of authentic pastoral work. In a generation rife with celebrity pastors, high-powered personalities, and pop culture-saturated preaching, Fuller reminds us that effective ministry puts character over charisma, piety over personality, and godliness over greatness. This is a book for our times.

Pastor David Daniels, Fellowship of Evangelical Baptist

Churches in Canada, Brooklin, Ontario

Table of contents

Illustrations

Foreword

I had just read a book by a man called Michael Haykin that was entitled *One Heart and One Soul: John Sutcliff of Olney, His Friends and His Times* (Evangelical Press, 1994). I cannot remember precisely when I read it, or who gave me the book, though I do remember it was a gift. I also remember the effect of the book. I knew I needed to know more about this group of brothers. I felt as if they were breathing the air that I was breathing, or—at the very least—the air that I wanted to breathe. They felt like new-discovered friends. Sutcliff, Ryland, Carey, Pearce, Fuller ... I began to look for more.

Not long afterwards I was standing in a book shop in London. There before me on the shelf were three volumes, beautifully bound in rich green cloth: the Sprinkle edition of *The Complete Works of Andrew Fuller* (1988). I barely hesitated over the investment. I plunged my hand into my pocket and then my head and heart into the first volume containing "Memoirs, Sermons, etc." I was deeply moved by Fuller's life and profoundly impressed by the sermons and letters that I read.

I continued to read. I hope that I not only learned about, but also that I learned from, these men of God. I found men who were far from perfect, and who never pretended to be, but who were full of God's Spirit and committed to the honour of Christ. As time passed, I had several happy opportunities to spend time with Michael Haykin, and to swap thoughts and stories and discoveries with him about our mutual friends.

Then, a few years ago, I was speaking with my friend, Brian Croft, about a potential reading scheme for his upcoming sabbatical. Who might you read? What about Andrew Fuller? Where to begin? The sermons! Since then we have often spoken with gratitude of the benefits we have enjoyed from diving into these sweet waters.

It is, therefore, with some pleasure that I write the foreword to this book, with its pleasing intertwining of friends and subjects. You have spiritual gold in your hand.

Andrew Fuller's 'ordination sermons' have been a happy source of fruitful contemplation for many. They are not written from the academic's ivory tower, but neither are they the ignorant musings of a thoughtless man. They are not heartless and high-minded theories, but the heartfelt exhortations of a man deeply interested in the people to whom and the churches to which he is preaching, and in the progress of the heavenly kingdom of which he is a humble part.

They are written by a man who has wrestled with God. They are written out of the crucible of a life of labour for the Lord, with a generous share of trials and troubles. They are products of the experience and the struggles of consistent pastoral endeavour. They are written by a man who smells of sheep, a man who has got his hands dirty tending God's flock. And they are so written that they are just as useful today as they ever were when he first preached them.

Andrew Fuller will speak to you as a man before he speaks to you as a minister. He will be concerned with your walk with Christ before he turns his attention to your work for Christ. He sounds notes which are too much neglected in modern works about pastoral ministry, taken up as they often are with systems and programs. He has an appetite for the genuinely needful rather than the apparently functional. He is concerned more for substance than with appearance, more for the spiritual vitality of a man than with anything else.

Remember that Fuller was a plain man. You should not proceed unless you are ready for some plain speaking. Fuller was a serious man. You should not proceed unless you are ready for some painful searching. Fuller was an earnest man. You should not proceed unless you are willing to be stirred and moved. This servant of Christ will not lead you into the playground but he will guide you across the battleground.

It is my hope that this study of Fuller's sermons to preachers will be of real help to new generations of men who are seeking to serve God. I believe that you will find within these pages a wise guide whose powerful voice, sounding down through the centuries, will be a blessing to each reader. I trust that the warnings of these pages will keep your feet from straying into dangerous ways. I trust that the exhortations of these pages will direct you to run with perseverance in paths of righteousness. I trust that the encouragements of these pages will strengthen your hand in the work that you have been given to do.

I hope that you will find here a true friend, a real counsellor, and a faithful mentor. I am glad for the work that has been done in putting these sermons before you in an accessible form.

One of Fuller's favourite divine maxims was drawn from the tenth verse of Ecclesiastes 9: "Whatever your hand finds to do, do it with your might." My prayer will be that, in reading these sermons and the accompanying essays and notes, you will catch something of the spirit of Fuller and his friends, and so learn to serve our Lord and Saviour Jesus Christ with all your might.

Jeremy Walker

Abbreviations

Complete Works *The Complete Works of the Rev. Andrew Fuller*, ed. Joseph Belcher (1845 ed.; repr. Harrisonburg, VA: Sprinkle Publications, 1988), 3 volumes.

To Matthew J. Hall and Hershael W. York
for their fine leadership in
the School of Theology
at
The Southern Baptist Theological Seminary

Introduction

Evangelical pastoral ministry is in crisis. Since the Sixties, various pastoral models have been tried and found wanting, and none more so than the celebrity mega-church pastor, which has recently been at the heart of serious questions being raised about the integrity of Evangelicalism in North America. A key part of the solution to this crisis is found in the admonition of Hebrews 13:7, where the recipients of that ancient, yet timeless, letter are urged first to 'remember [their] leaders, those who spoke to [them] the Word of God', then to reflect deeply on the 'way of life' of these leaders, and finally to 'imitate their faith' (ESV). The author of Hebrews assumes that Christian communities are to be communities of memory, where, among other things, the lives and thought of past Christian leaders are not only recalled but also used as models of faithful leadership in the present. In essence, this is what has come to be called *ressourcement*, or the retrieval of the riches of church history for life and direction in the present. When it comes to pastoral leadership there are many models of faithful ministry in the history of the church, men like Basil of Caesarea and John Wycliffe, Richard Greenham and Charles Simeon. This book is focused on the pastoral model primarily found in nineteen ordination sermons of the pastor-theologian Andrew Fuller (1754–1815). It is an exercise in pastoral *ressourcement*, in which Fuller's thinking about and practice of pastoral ministry is shown to be quite germane for modern-day ministers and congregations.

'The elephant of Kettering'

In the century following the death of Andrew Fuller (1754–1815) many Christians well knew the worth of this Baptist pastor-theologian. Welsh author David Phillips described him as the 'elephant of Kettering,' an allusion to his weighty theological influence in both his own day and the decades following his decease.[1] Forty years later, the celebrated Baptist preacher Charles Haddon Spurgeon (1834–1892) told Fuller's last surviving son, Andrew Gunton Fuller, after he had read the latter's biography of his father:

> I have long considered your father to be the greatest theologian of the century, and I do not know that your pages have made me think more highly of him as a divine than I had thought before. But I now see him within doors far more accurately, and see about the Christian man a soft radiance of tender love which had never been revealed to me either by former biographies or by his writings.[2]

And in the first decade of the twentieth century, Southern

---

1 David Phillips, *Memoir of the Life, Labors, and Extensive Usefulness of the Rev. Christmas Evans* (New York, NY: M. W. Dodd, 1843), 74. Fuller was the pastor of the Baptist church in Kettering from 1782 till his death in 1815.

For the life and ministry of Fuller, see especially Peter J. Morden, *The Life and Thought of Andrew Fuller (1754–1815)* (Milton Keynes, England: Paternoster, 2015). For a briefer study, see Gilbert S. Laws, *Andrew Fuller: Pastor, Theologian, Ropeholder* (London: Carey Press, 1942); John Piper, *Andrew Fuller: Holy Faith, Worthy Gospel, World Mission* (Wheaton, IL: Crossway, 2016). Also see the excellent study of Fuller's theology, known in his own day as 'Fullerism', by E.F. Clipsham, 'Andrew Fuller and Fullerism: A Study in Evangelical Calvinism', *The Baptist Quarterly*, 20 (1963–1964): 99–114, 146–154, 214–225, 268–276.

2 Cited Laws, *Andrew Fuller*, 127.

Baptist historian A.H. Newman, who taught church history at McMaster University in Ontario from 1881 to 1901, commented that Fuller's influence for good on American Baptists was 'incalculable.'[3] And more recently, Timothy George has noted that Fuller is 'the most influential Baptist theologian between John Bunyan' in the seventeenth century and our day.[4]

Fuller published major theological works on a variety of issues, many of them in the area of apologetics. He wrote decisive rebuttals of such eighteenth-century theological aberrations as hyper-Calvinism and Sandemanianism, penned an influential refutation of Socinianism (or Unitarianism), and in 1799 authored the definitive eighteenth-century Baptist response to Deism.[5] Most significantly, Fuller's evangelical Calvinism, known as 'Fullerism' even in his day, was a key theological voice in the genesis of the modern missionary movement. In the words of E.F. Clipsham: 'The greatest merit of "Fullerism" [...] is that it provided the theological basis for the missionary movement of [William] Carey, and for the evangelical outreach of the churches at home. It

---

3 'Fuller, Andrew' in Samuel Macauley Jackson, *et al.* ed., *The New Schaff-Herzog Encyclopaedia of Religious Knowledge* (New York, NY/London: Funk and Wagnalls Co., 1909), 4:409.

4 Endorsement of Peter J. Morden, *Offering Christ to the World: Andrew Fuller (1754–1815) and the Revival of Eighteenth Century Particular Baptist Life* (Carlisle: Paternoster, 2003). The authors are indebted to Jeremy Walker, ' "On the Side of God": Andrew Fuller's Pastoral Theology" in *The Power of God* ([London]: Westminster Conference, 2015), 8, for this reference.

5 Fuller's response to hyper-Calvinism was his *The Gospel Worthy of All Acceptation*, which first appeared in 1785. The second edition of this work, published in 1801, can be found in *Complete Works*, II, 328–416. For his reply to Sandemanianism, see *Strictures on Sandemanianism, in Twelve Letters to a Friend* (*Complete Works*, II, 561–646). His chief response to Socinianism was *The Particular and Socinian Systems Examined and Compared, as to their Moral Tendency* (*Complete Works*, II, 108–242). And his key refutation of Deism, especially that of the popularizer Thomas Paine (1737–1809), was *The Gospel Its Own Witness* (*Complete Works*, II, 1–107).

The three-volume edition of Fuller's works will be cited throughout this book as simply *Complete Works* with the respective volume and pages.

showed the compatibility of evangelical missionary endeavour with Calvinistic theology.'[6] And as Philip Roberts, one-time President of Midwestern Baptist Theological Seminary, has observed:

> [Fuller] helped to link the earlier Baptists, whose chief concern was the establishment of ideal New Testament congregations, with those in the nineteenth century driven to make the gospel known worldwide. His contribution helped to guarantee that many of the leading Baptists of the 1800s would typify fervent evangelism and world missions. [...] Without his courage and doctrinal integrity in the face of what he considered to be theological aberrations, the Baptist mission movement might have been stillborn.[7]

Alongside his incisive apologetic works and this ideological commitment to and passionate involvement in mission, Fuller was also a pastor. His pastoral ministry began in Soham, near Cambridge, in 1775, where he successfully transcended a hyper-Calvinistic environment. From there he moved to Kettering, Northamptonshire, in 1782, where he served as the main preacher and pastor to a growing congregation. In 1810, he testified, 'I have been pastor of the church which I now serve for nearly thirty years, without a single difference.'[8] During his thirty-three years at Kettering, from 1782 to 1815, the membership of the church more than doubled (from 88 to 174) and the number of 'hearers' was often over a thousand, necessitating several additions to the church building. Perusal of his vast correspondence—most of which is housed in the Angus Library, Regent's Park College, at the University of Oxford—reveals that Fuller was first and foremost a

---

6 Clipsham, *Andrew Fuller and Fullerism* 100.

7 Phil Roberts, 'Andrew Fuller' in Timothy George and David S. Dockery, ed., *Theologians of the Baptist Tradition* (Rev. ed.; Nashville, TN: Broadman & Holman, 2001), 46–47. See below for details of Fuller's missional activism, pages 78–83.

8 Andrew Fuller, 'Counsels to a Young Minister in Prospect of Ordination' (*Complete Works*, III, 497; see below, Appendix 1). For this quote and much of this paragraph, the authors are indebted to Walker, 'On the Side of God', 8.

pastor. And though he did not always succeed, he was constantly fighting to ensure that his many other responsibilities did not encroach upon those related to the pastorate.

Two examples depict his pastoral heart. After Fuller died, there was found among his possessions a small book entitled *Families who attend at the Meeting, August, 1788*. In it, he wrote: 'A Review of these may assist me in praying and preaching.'[9] Then, among his letters there is one dated February 8, 1812, which was written to a wayward member of his flock. In it, Fuller laid bare his pastor's heart when he stated:

> When a parent loses [...] a child nothing but the recovery of that child can heal the wound. If he could have many other children, that would not do it [...] Thus it is with me towards you. Nothing but your return to God and the Church can heal the wound.[10]

Fuller's pastoral heart is also clearly seen in his ordination sermons, a good number of which are reproduced in this volume. Here, Fuller lays out what is essentially a manual of pastoralia. There are twenty-nine of Fuller's ordination sermons extant. They comprise both sermons to the ordinands and to the congregations among whom they would serve. Seventeen sermons included in this book are the extant sermons that he preached to ordinands (three of them were addressed to both the ordinand and the congregation). The other two addresses in this book were given to ministerial students at the two Baptist schools in southern England, Bristol Baptist Academy and Stepney Academical Institution in London and are included as they represent Fuller's mature thought about pastoral ministry (both were given in the last

---

9 Gladys M. Barrett, *A Brief History of Fuller Church, Kettering* ([St. Albans, Hertfordshire, *c.*1946]), 9.

10 Barrett, *Brief History of Fuller Church*, 9.

six years of Fuller's life).[11] There are also two important letters to younger pastors, also written by Fuller in 1810, that contain wisdom regarding pastoral authority and sexual purity.[12] These letters can be found as the first two Appendices. The sermons comprise Part II of this book and have been edited by Michael Haykin.

Preceding these sermons is what the authors are calling 'Part I: Historical considerations.' This portion of the book contains two historical studies: Ian Clary and Michael Haykin sketch the history of ordination sermons in the larger historical context of Fuller's Baptist community, namely, English Dissent in the long eighteenth century; then, Haykin provides the reader with an overview of Fuller's perspective on what constitutes faithful pastoral ministry. Typical of his Reformed tradition, marked as it was by a spirituality of the Word, was Fuller's conviction that preaching is 'the leading duty of a minister.'[13] Since this area of Fuller's thinking about pastoral ministry has been sufficiently

---

11 Two of the sermons included among Fuller's ordination sermons are addresses to missionaries sent out by the Baptist Missionary Society in the 1790s, one of whom was Fuller's close friend William Carey. See *Complete Works*, I, 510–515.

12 The letter on sexual purity is unknown, probably even to most Fuller scholars, as it has lain buried in an obscure nineteenth-century journal.

13 Andrew Fuller, *Ministers and Churches Exhorted to Serve One Another in Love* (*Complete Works*, I, 544; below, page 197). Here, Fuller reflects his tradition. For example, in the association records of the Northern Baptist Association, which was composed of Baptist churches in the old English counties of Northumberland, Cumberland, Westmoreland, and Durham, the following answer was given to a question raised in 1701 as to who may administer the ordinances of the Lord's Supper and Baptism: 'Those persons that the Church approves of to preach the Gospel we think it safe to approve likewise for the administering other ordinances, preaching being the greater work.' In 1703, when a similar question was asked, it was stated that 'those whom the Church approves to preach the Gospel may also administer the ordinances of baptism and the Lord's Supper, preaching being the main and principal work of the Gospel' (S. L. Copson, *Association Life of the Particular Baptists of Northern England 1699–1732* [London: Baptist Historical Society, 1991], 89, 95).

explored in various articles, the focus of Haykin's overview is Fuller's depiction of the character and affections of the minister.[14]

The final portion of the book, 'Part III: Modern pastoral applications' has been written by Brian Croft with the help of Jeremy Walker; both of whom are experienced pastors. This section of the book seeks to demonstrate how Fuller's pastoral theology is an excellent model for pastors today and his advice still very germane.

It is the ardent prayer of all of those involved in the writing of this work that our great God use it for his glory and his Church's good!

The authors are indebted to the fine editorial work of Graham Hind and Digby James in making this book possible, and also to the help of Dustin Benge with the cover.

---

14 For Fuller as a preacher, see Edwin Charles Dargan, *A History of Preaching* (New York: Hodder & Stoughton/George H. Doran Co., 1912), II, 332–333; Harlice E. Keown, 'The Preaching of Andrew Fuller' (ThM thesis, Southern Baptist Theological Seminary, 1957); Thomas R. McKibbens, Jr., *The Forgotten Heritage: A Lineage of Great Baptist Preaching* (Macon, GA: Mercer University Press, 1986), 44–52; Paul Brewster, *Andrew Fuller: Model Pastor-Theologian* (Nashville, TN: B&H Publishing, 2010), 110–120; Keith S. Grant, 'Plain, Evangelical, and Affectionate: The Preaching of Andrew Fuller (1754–1815)', *Crux*, 48, no.1 (Spring 2012): 12–22; *idem, Andrew Fuller and the Evangelical Renewal of Pastoral Theology*, Studies in Baptist History and Thought, vol.36 (Milton Keynes: Paternoster, 2013), 77–104; Jeremy Walker, '"On the Side of God": Andrew Fuller's Pastoral Theology' in *The Power of God* ([London]: Westminster Conference, 2015), 21–28; Michael A.G. Haykin, 'The Power of Preaching: The Presence of the Holy Spirit' in Joel R. Beeke and Dustin W. Benge, ed., *Pulpit Aflame: Essays in Honor of Steven J. Lawson* (Grand Rapids, MI: Reformation Heritage Books, 2016), 131–141.

For Fuller's thoughts on preaching in these ordination sermons, see especially *The Nature of the Gospel, and Manner in Which It Ought to Be Preached* (*Complete Works*, I, 494–496; below, pages 145–150); *idem, Preaching Christ* (*Complete Works*, I, 501–504; below, pages 161–167); *idem, Affectionate Concern of a Minister for the Salvation of his Hearers* (*Complete Works*, I, 509–510; below, pages 178–180); *idem, Faith in the Gospel a Necessary Prerequisite to Preaching It* (*Complete Works*, I, 515–517; below, pages 181–186).

Notes on the text

The text of Fuller's sermons is that found in the first volume of the standard three-volume edition printed in 1845 by the American Baptist Publication Society and reprinted in the 1980s: *The Complete Works of the Rev. Andrew Fuller*, ed. Joseph Belcher (1845 ed.; repr. Harrisonburg, VA: Sprinkle Publications, 1988). Scripture references not noted by Fuller have been placed in footnotes. Only clear citations have been noted, not the many allusions that fill Fuller's sermons. The modern method of citing biblical references with Arabic numerals has also been adopted, which entailed changing Fuller's references that used Roman numerals for the chapter designations. Punctuation and capitalization have been modernized, as has the term 'etc.' A few early nineteenth-century spellings have also been changed, and the terms 'Gospel', 'Scripture', 'Bible', and 'Word' (when it refers to the Scriptures) consistently capitalized. The text of the Scriptures cited in Part III is the New American Standard Bible. However, the phrase, 'Take heed to yourself and the flock' comes from the King James Version and New King James Version.

Andrew Fuller timeline

Compiled by Ian H. Clary

1754 February 6 Fuller born at Wicken, Cambridgeshire

Jonathan Edwards' *Freedom of the Will* published

1761 Moved to Soham with family

1769 November Conversion

1770 Baptized in Soham; joined Particular Baptist church in Soham, which was pastored by John Eve

1775 May 3 Ordained pastor of church in Soham

1776 Married Sarah Gardiner of Burwell, Cambridgeshire

1782 October Moved to Kettering to pastor the Particular Baptist church

1784 June Northamptonshire Association issued the "Call to Prayer"

1785 *The Gospel Worthy of All Acceptation* published

1792 August 23 Wife Sarah died

October Particular Baptist Society for Propagating of the Gospel Among the Heathen formed, later to be called the Baptist Missionary Society; Fuller appointed its first secretary

1793 June William Carey, his family, and John Thomas sent to India by the Baptist Missionary Society

1794 December 30 Married Ann Coles of Ampthill, Bedfordshire

1798 Awarded an honorary Doctor of Divinity from Princeton University

1800 *Memoir of the Rev. Samuel Pearce* published

1805 Awarded an honorary Doctor of Divinity from Yale University

1810 *Strictures on Sandemanianism* published

1811 John Keen Hall appointed as Fuller's assistant

1815 May 7 Fuller died in Kettering

Part I: Historical considerations

Geo. Vertue ad Vivum   delin et Sculpsit

Matthæus Henry V.D.M.

Matthew Henry

Chapter 1: An historical survey of the ordination sermon in eighteenth-century English Dissent

The preaching of Scripture has always been an essential element of Christian worship. As O. C. Edwards, Jr., stated in his monumental history of the subject: 'There is no activity more characteristic of the church than preaching.'[1] We see the truth of this played out in the life of the New Testament church from the first Christian sermon preached by Peter in Acts 2 to Paul's injunction to his confidant Timothy in 1 Timothy 4:2, where he tells his younger ministry partner to 'preach the word in season and out of season.' This apostolic emphasis on preaching also played a major role in English church history. As Raymond Brown has observed, 'In any account of religious life and thought in post-reformation England it is almost impossible to exaggerate the influence of the sermon.'[2] For example, in a diary entry for February 5, 1781, Andrew Fuller described preaching thus:

---

1 O. C. Edwards Jr., *A History of Preaching* (Nashville, TN: Abingdon Press, 2004), 1:3.

2 Raymond Brown, 'Baptist Preaching in Early 18th Century England', *The Baptist Quarterly*, 31, no. 1 (January 1985). Christopher J. Ellis rightly speaks of the 'dominance

A pulpit seems an awful place! An opportunity for addressing a company of mortals on their eternal interests. Oh how important! We preach for eternity. We, in a sense, are set for the rising and falling of many in Israel. And our own rise and fall is equally therein involved.[3]

Fuller exemplified this sentiment in his own ministry at both Soham and Kettering, and, as evident in this volume, it was regularly expressed in his sermons to ordinands to the Baptist ministry. For instance, in a sermon entitled *Pastors Required to Feed the Flock of Christ*, which was based on John 11:16, Fuller reminded the new minister of Christ's love for his people as 'Chief Shepherd' and explained that his duty was to 'feed' them as a shepherd feeds his sheep. By implication, Fuller was heightening the importance of preaching, connecting the work of the preacher to that of Christ in his office as The Good Shepherd. But the 'oversight' that Fuller highlighted goes beyond the ministry of the Word and includes ruling, protecting, and caring for the sheep more generally. And key to this oversight was the minister's character.[4]

Christian ministry and personal godliness are intimately yoked together in a number of New Testament writings. Paul's list of qualifications for an elder in 1 Timothy 3:1–13, for instance, are predominantly character-based. In keeping with this train of thought—godliness and pastoral ministry—this chapter will outline the emphasis that English Dissent in the long eighteenth century placed on the character of a minister as integral to the discharge of pastoral duties. Of course, this is not the only theme

---

of preaching in Baptist worship' (*Gathering: A Theology and Spirituality of Worship in Free Church Tradition* [London: SCM Press, 2004], 134). See also Ellis' whole chapter on the role of preaching in Baptist worship: *Gathering*, 124–149.

3 Andrew Fuller, *The Diary of Andrew Fuller, 1780–1801*, ed. Michael D. McMullen and D. Timothy Whelan, *The Complete Works of Andrew Fuller*, vol.1 (Berlin: Walter de Gruyter, 2016), 24.

4 Andrew Fuller, *Pastors Required to Feed the Flock of Christ* (*Complete Works*, I, 477–478; below, pages 109–110).

to appear in this tradition's ordination sermons. Issues such as calling, the practical duties of ministry, and the need for sound doctrine were also regularly expressed by preachers at ordinations. These other themes will be noted but the focus of this chapter will be on the encouragement to godliness found in ordination sermons as they were preached by English Dissenting ministers. This provides a historical background to Fuller's own understanding of a godly ministry.

The sampling in this chapter will be limited but representative. After a quick look at the history and nature of English Dissent, the importance of ordination sermons for this tradition is considered, and then ordination sermons from three representative ministers— the Presbyterian Matthew Henry (1662–1714), the Particular Baptist John Gill (1697–1771), and the Congregationalist Philip Doddridge (1702–1751)—will be examined with regard to their thinking about the character of the pastor.

English Dissent—what is it?

Elizabeth I was content with a church that was 'Calvinistic in theology, [but] Erastian in Church order and government [i.e. the state was ascendant over the church in these areas], and largely mediaeval in liturgy.'[5] In response to this ecclesiastical 'settledness', there arose the Puritan movement in the early 1560s, which sought to reform the Elizabethan church after the model of the churches in Protestant Switzerland, especially those in Geneva and Zürich.[6] Initially, Puritan concerns were centred on the reform of the Church's worship and liturgy. In the 1570s and 1580s, however, the ecclesiological positions known as Presbyterianism and Congregationalism were developed by Puritan authors,

---

5 Robert C. Walton, *The Gathered Community* (London: Carey Press, 1946), 59.

6 Defining Puritanism is notoriously difficult. See Ian Hugh Clary, 'Hot Protestants: A Taxonomy of English Puritanism', *Puritan Reformed Journal* 2, no.1 (January 2010): 41–66.

and the quarrel between the Puritans and those who were quite content with the Church of England as it was (later known by the term 'Anglican') broadened to include matters relating to church government. It was during the 1580s and 1590s that some radical Puritans, despairing of a full reformation within the Church of England, began to separate from the state church and organize their own Separatist congregations. During the British Civil Wars (1638–1651), yet more Puritans left the state church to set up their own churches, and after the Restoration of the monarchy in 1662, a large number of ministers—possibly as many as a quarter of the ministers of the Church of England—were expelled by the Act of Uniformity, an event that came to be known as the 'Great Ejection.'[7] Thus, various streams of Separatism and Puritanism fed into what came to be known as Dissent or Nonconformity, which essentially coalesced in three major denominational bodies: the Presbyterians, Congregationalists, and the Particular Baptists.[8]

An interesting, though brief, sketch of the characteristics of the Dissenting movement were traced out in a letter prefixed to an ordination sermon preached in 1736 by Edmund Calamy IV (c.1697–1755). A Presbyterian minister and historian, Calamy's grandfather, also named Edmund, suffered for his Nonconformity in the Great Ejection. It is worth examining the younger Calamy's *A Letter to a Divine in Germany* as it was published only twenty years before Fuller's birth in 1754, and is representative of the way Nonconformists viewed themselves in that day. The sermon to

---

7 For two contemporary perspectives on the 'Great Ejection', see Gary Brady, *The Great Ejection 1662: Today's Evangelicalism Rooted in Puritan Persecution* (Darlington, UK: EP Books, 2012) and Lee Gatiss, *The Tragedy of 1662: The Ejection and Persecution of the Puritans*, Latimer Studies Book 66 (London: Latimer Trust, 2007).

8 The definitive history of the Dissenters from the time of the Reformation remains Michael R. Watts, *The Dissenters*, 3 vols. (Oxford: Oxford University Press, 1986–2015). For the origin of the Particular and General Baptists in English Puritanism, see Michael A. G. Haykin, *Kiffin, Knollys and Keach: Rediscovering our English Baptist Heritage* (Darlington, UK: Evangelical Press, 1997).

which the letter was attached was preached at the ordination of Samuel Chandler (c. 1693–1766), also a Presbyterian minister and a pamphleteer, who often courted controversy with his apparently aberrant Christology. Calamy began the letter on Dissent by explaining that many in the sixteenth century had desired that 'the worship and government of the Church might be more agreeable to the Holy Scriptures, and the methods of other Protestant Churches: And they are still as desirous of it as ever, tho' they have not hitherto been able to obtain it.'[9] Calamy surveyed the theme of the persecution of Dissent through the various monarchs of the Tudor and Stuart eras, up to the then-more recent era of Queen Anne when Dissenters were

> incapacitated from holding any place of profit or trust under the government. [...] They have also been by law denied the liberty of educating their own children, than which they could not well have been exposed to a greater hardship, or been brought under a more disheartening mark of distinction.[10]

Of their theological distinctives, Calamy noted the general differences between the Presbyterians and Congregationalists pertaining to church government, and also observed the further difference over the sacrament of baptism between the Presbyterians and Congregationalists, on the one hand, and the Baptists, on the other. Calamy then provided the German recipient of his letter with a general summary of what a Dissenting church service might look like, in which there was a simplified order of the preached Word, the sacraments of baptism and communion, alms giving, and catechetical instruction. One key difference between the state church and Dissent that Calamy emphasized was the right of each Dissenting congregation to choose its own minister. Calamy

---

9 Edmund Calamy, *A Letter to a Divine in Germany, Giving a Brief, but True, Account of the Protestant Dissenters in England* (London: Richard Hett, 1736), 3.

10 Calamy, *Letter to a Divine in Germany*, 7.

also highlighted the importance that Dissenters placed on the relationship between godliness and pastoral ministry. He described what was to happen if a minister fell into sin:

> When ministers prove scandalous, their people look upon themselves as at liberty to desert them; and the neighbouring ministers taking cognizance of such matters, are ready to admonish them so to do, and to encourage them in it, if there be no reformation, or if the scandals were of such a nature, as not to be repair'd without a remaining blemish to the sacred ministry.'[11]

In this text, Calamy, not only brought to the fore the greater degree of autonomy that Dissenting churches had in governance relative to the Church of England, but he also underlined the importance that Dissenters placed on the character of the minister. If the pastor fell into sin or drifted into theological error, he was to be removed by the congregation with the help of neighbouring churches.

The nature and importance of ordination sermons

Sermons were an ubiquitous part of the world of eighteenth-century England. As such, it is surprising that literature on the history of preaching from this period is relatively sparse in its evaluation of ordination sermons. In her otherwise outstanding analysis of sermonic literature preached in eighteenth-century London, Jennifer Farooq hardly touches on the ordination sermon.[12] She is not alone, as a survey of other standard works on the sermon from the period also lack serious engagement with these rich texts.[13] Such a lacuna is strange because this

---

11 Calamy, *Letter to a Divine in Germany*, 14–15.

12 Jennifer Farooq, *Preaching in Eighteenth-Century London*, Studies in Modern British Religious History, vol. 30 (Woodbridge, Suffolk: The Boydell Press, 2013).

13 See, for example, Peter McCullough, Hugh Adlington, and Emma Rhatigan, eds., *The Oxford Handbook of the Early Modern Sermon* (Oxford: Oxford University

homiletical genre provides a wealth of information about the way that Dissenters understood pastoral ministry. Ordination sermons regularly describe the ideals of pastoral ministry, addressed from one pastor to another as well as charges given to the congregation that the ordinand would pastor. While there are texts such as John Gill's *A Complete Body of Doctrinal and Practical Divinity* (1769–1770) that outline an Evangelical and Reformed pastoral theology in systematic detail, the added value of ordination sermons is their demonstration of what that pastoral theology looked like on the ground in the eighteenth century. As Nigel Wheeler has rightly observed, 'ordination sermons were delivered by active practitioners who were directly addressing other practicing pastors with the fervor of a *shared* special interest in a divine cause.'[14] They make a unique contribution not only to eighteenth-century sermons as a genre, but also to the understanding of Evangelical pastoral theology.

The context in which ordination sermons and charges were given is also noteworthy. In Wheeler's words:

> [T]he solemn designation of a pastor to the ministry occurred in the public milieu of a local church as the charge was delivered in a covenantal context. This exchange between practitioners was expressed openly. The church and their newly ordained pastor were voluntarily binding themselves together in a covenantal relationship that produced an increased accountability and commitment towards one another. For the pastor especially this necessitated the manifestation of a blameless character. It was the pastor's duty to admonish people to obey certain theological precepts to which he, as both a Christian and member of the church, was also accountable. In this role, where his life was regularly exposed to sustained public

---

Press, 2011) and Keith A. Francis and William Gibson, eds., *Oxford Handbook of the British Sermon 1689–1901* (Oxford: Oxford University Press, 2012).

14 Nigel Wheeler, 'Andrew Fuller's Ordination Sermons', *Eusebeia* 8 (Spring 2008): 170.

scrutiny, any discrepancies between his words and actions were amplified. As a leader he had an even greater responsibility than the average church member to maintain a consistent example of practicing what he preached.[15]

In Baptist circles specifically, along with the ordination sermon, there would normally be a charge to the congregation as to how they should conduct themselves with regard to their pastor, prayer for the pastor with the laying-on-of-hands by other elders present,[16] recitation of a confession of faith drawn up by the ordinand, and congregational singing.[17]

The following reflection on ordination sermons from three

---

15 Nigel David Wheeler, 'Eminent Spirituality and Eminent Usefulness: Andrew Fuller's (1754–1815) Pastoral Theology in his Ordination Sermons' (PhD thesis, University of Pretoria, 2009), 80.

16 As Stephen Copson comments with regard to the understanding of this rite among the Baptists of this era: 'The laying of hands was a demonstrative act, which did not confer any special qualities or pass on authority in itself' ('Two Ordinations at Bridlington in 1737', *The Baptist Quarterly*, 33 [1989]: 146).

17 See, for example, these various elements in *A Charge and Sermon together with an Introductory Discourse and Confession of Faith Delivered at the Ordination of the Rev. Mr. Abraham Booth Feb.16, 1769, in Goodman's Fields* (London, 1769); Andrew Fuller and John Ryland, *The Qualifications and Encouragement of a faithful Minister, illustrated by the Character and Success of Barnabas. And, Paul's Charge to the Corinthians respecting their Treatment of Timothy, applied to the Conduct of Churches toward Their Pastors. Being the Substance of Two Discourses, Delivered at The Settlement of The Rev. Mr. Robert Fawkner, in the Pastoral Office, Over the Baptist Church at Thorn, in Bedfordshire, October 31, 1787* (London: Thorn Baptist Church, 1787); Copson, 'Two Ordinations', 146; and 'Appendix 3: William Carey's summary of his ordination.' See also Philip Doddridge, 'An Appendix relating to the Usual Methods of Ordination amongst the Protestant Dissenters' in *The Works of Philip Doddridge, D.D.*, 5 vols. (London: W. J. and J. Richardson, *et al.*, 1803–1804), 4:270–276. This appendix is also reprinted in Alan P. F. Sell, David J. Hall, and Ian Sellers, *Protestant Nonconformist Texts Volume 2: The Eighteenth Century* (Eugene, OR: Wipf & Stock Publishers, 2015), 163–167. It is noteworthy that, whereas Presbyterian ordinands would affirm their commitment to the Westminster Standards, Congregationalist (or Independent) and Particular Baptist candidates for pastoral ministry crafted their own confessions of faith.

important, and representative eighteenth-century Nonconformist ministers—Henry, Gill, and Doddridge—demonstrates that Andrew Fuller's ordination addresses are firmly in line with this tradition of Dissenting pastoral theology and its concern for ministerial character.[18]

Matthew Henry—'ministers must not live to themselves'

Alongside the seventeenth-century work of Matthew Poole (1624–1679), arguably the most important commentary on Scripture to come out of early modern England is the six-volume *An Exposition of the Old and New Testaments* (1708–1710), which was penned by the Puritan Matthew Henry.[19] Still in print today, this classic work is effectively a compendium of English Reformed commentary on nearly every book of the Bible up to his day and as such exemplifies how the Puritan tradition generally read Scripture.[20]

---

18 Of course, eighteenth-century Dissenters were not the only ones concerned with ministerial holiness—a survey of Evangelical Anglican ordination sermons would reveal similar themes. Themes of ministerial character drawn from ordination sermons thus announce another potential area of exploration for Dissenting catholicity in general, and in the case of Fuller, another avenue of what some are calling Baptist catholicity. See, for example, Steven R. Harmon, *Towards a Baptist Catholicity: Essays on Tradition and the Baptist Vision*, Studies in Baptist History and Thought, vol. 27 (Eugene, OR: Wipf & Stock Publishers, 2006).

19 Matthew Henry, *An Exposition of the Old and New Testaments in Six Volumes* (Edinburgh: Bell, Bradfute, Dickson and McCleish, 1791). Henry completed all of the Old Testament and the New Testament up to the Acts of the Apostles before his death in 1714. For Henry see Allan Harman, *Matthew Henry: His Life and Influence* (Fearn, Ross-Shire: Christian Focus, 2012); Paul Middleton and Matthew A. Collins, *Matthew Henry: The Bible, Prayer, and Piety: A Tercentenary Appreciation* (London: Bloomsbury, 2019).

20 Biblical scholar Brevard Childs has given good advice on how to make the best use of commentaries by older writers like Poole or Henry: 'I would strongly recommend that pastors secure one of the great English pastors who wrote commentaries on the whole Bible—namely, Matthew Henry, Thomas Scott, and Adam Clarke. One should not settle for an abbreviated modern edition, but should purchase the unabridged edition on the secondhand-book market. Needless to say,

His work functioned as a bridge between the Puritan era and
the Evangelicalism of the eighteenth century. We know from
the list of his library that Andrew Fuller had four of Henry's
writings, including the *Exposition*.[21] Allan Harman has attributed
the widespread importance of Henry's commentary to its intended
use for 'ordinary Christians, not learned scholars.'[22] Its readability
led to its popularity and longevity. This commentary was based
upon Henry's sermons preached at his church each Sunday, both
morning and evening, beginning in 1704. Following his analysis
of Henry's preaching as found in his *Exposition*, Hughes Oliphant
Old described Henry as 'a preacher who had the soul of a poet.'[23]

Though born in Wales, Henry was a Presbyterian pastor who
spent the bulk of his ministry in Chester while the latter years of
his life were spent pastoring in London. His father, Philip Henry
(1632–1696), had been a Church of England minister but was
ejected from his pulpit in Flintshire in 1661, a year before the Great
Ejection. The elder Henry had been trained at Oxford University
under the leadership of the famous Puritan theologian John Owen
(1616–1683). Philip would have a tremendous formative influence
on his son, particularly with regard to his Puritan theology
and Nonconformist ecclesiology.[24] After the restoration of the
monarchy, Oxford and Cambridge Universities barred Dissenters

---

the modern reader must exercise skill and acute discernment in using these volumes.
These old books can work as a trap and deception if the pastor is simply looking for a
retreat into the past, but if they are correctly used, innumerable riches can be tapped.'
See his Brevard Childs, *Old Testament Books for Pastor and Teacher* (Philadelphia, PA:
Westminster Press, 1977), 30.

21 Fuller, *Diary of Andrew Fuller, 1780–1801*, 216.

22 Allan M. Harman, 'The Impact of Matthew Henry's *Exposition* on Eighteenth-
Century Christianity', *Evangelical Quarterly*, 82 (2010): 13.

23 Hughes Oliphant Old, *The Reading and Preaching of the Scriptures in the Worship
of the Christian Church. Volume 5: Moderatism, Pietism, and Awakening* (Grand Rapids,
MI: Wm. B. Eerdmans, 2004), 31.

24 For a helpful study of Philip Henry's life as a Nonconformist with attention
paid to his relationship to his son, see David L. Wykes, 'The Early Years of Religious

from graduating from their schools, so the younger Henry was educated by his father and then went on to Thomas Doolittle's (*c.*1632–1707) Dissenting academy in London. Henry also had some training in law at Gray's Inn in London in 1685. Two years later he became the minister at the Presbyterian church in Chester where he served for most of his life. He died in 1714 while on a trip from London to Chester.

William C. Watson and W. Ross Hastings list sixteen of Henry's published sermons; only two are ordination sermons.[25] Both were preached in 1712, during Henry's ministry in London, and just two years before his death. The first was preached in London on January 7, 1713 at the ordination of Benjamin Atkinson (*c.*1680–1765), who ministered in Cheapside.[26] Atkinson is best known for his contribution to the parts of the *Exposition* that Henry was unable to finish, namely, Acts to Revelation. Henry's second ordination sermon was preached for Samuel Clarke (1684–1750), the minister of the Nonconformist church at St. Albans.[27] The focus of what follows is on the sermon for Atkinson.

Henry chose Isaiah 6:8 as his text for Atkinson's ordination: 'Also I heard the voice of the Lord, saying, Whom shall I send, and who will go for us? Then said I, Here am I; send me.' In so doing, Henry drew an explicit link between the calling of the

---

Dissent in Cheshire Following James II's Declaration of Indulgence in April 1687', *Northern History*, 52, no.2 (September 2015): 217–232.

25 William C. Watson and W. Ross Hastings, 'Matthew Henry: Exegesis and Exposition for the Church and the Pulpit' in Benjamin K. Forrest, Kevin L. King Sr., Bill Curtis, and Dwayne Milioni, ed., *A Legacy of Preaching Volume 1: Apostles to the Revivalists: The Life, Theology, and Method of History's Great Preachers* (Grand Rapids, MI: Zondervan, 2018), 439.

26 Walter Wilson, *The History and Antiquities of Dissenting Churches and Meeting Houses, in London, Westminster, and Southwark*, 4 vols. (London: W. Button, 1808), 2:100–102.

27 Not to be confused with the philosopher and Arian theologian Samuel Clarke (1675–1729).

minister and the instructions given by Yahweh to the 'evangelical prophet.' Isaiah is called an 'evangelical' because, of all the prophets, '[he] spake so plainly and fully of Christ, and the grace of the gospel.'[28] The sermon begins by outlining the nature of the prophet's calling. This text was about Isaiah's 'public entry' into his mission, even though he had likely been a 'candidate' beforehand wherein he was 'tried' for ministry. A ministerial 'trial' was part of the ordination practice for Presbyterians. Part of the ordinand's spiritual preparation was a 'humbling sense of his own sinfulness', coupled with 'a comfortable sense of the pardon of sin', and an assurance of his acceptance with God.[29] Henry highlighted these two aspects for Atkinson's sake, so that he might be better prepared for ministry. He reminded the would-be minister that upon his commission, Isaiah was 'much affected' by his own sin before a holy God. But just as Isaiah was humbled, he was also exalted in order to be honoured for his calling. This was so because 'God looks upon those as fittest to be honoured by him, and employed for him, who are humbled and low in their own eyes.' It is God who fits for ministry, by instilling humility in his ministers. Henry here employs a Christological image that has direct bearing on his hearer: 'As Christ, so Christians, are first humbled, and then exalted; like a corn of wheat, die first, and then revive [...] Before honour is humility.'[30] This exaltation is a result of Isaiah's own assurance of pardon and his 'reconciliation to God.' The atoning coal from the altar that was laid upon the prophet's mouth was the ground of the promise that God would not 'ruin' Isaiah. Henry commented: 'They who are thus sprinkled from an evil conscience, are best prepared to serve the living God.' In terms of pastoral ministry, what this meant was that it was those 'who have known

---

28 Matthew Henry, *A Sermon, Preached at the Ordination of Mr. Atkinson* in *The Miscellaneous Works of the Rev. Matthew Henry* (London: Joseph Ogle Robinson, 1830), 967.

29 Henry, *Sermon*, 967.

30 Henry, *Sermon*, 968.

experimentally the power' of Christ crucified and are 'clothed with that everlasting righteousness' that Christ's death purchased who 'can best preach Christ crucified.'[31]

In the heart of the sermon, Henry reminded Atkinson that though ministers are of a lowly estate, they are sent by One who is 'enthroned' and 'greatly exalted' and thus God honours gospel ministers as his spokespersons.[32] And pointing to the plurality in the question, 'who will go for us?', Henry also observed that this One who sends is also Three.[33]

Henry now began to reflect upon the one who is called to ministry. He had much to say about this, including the ways that God calls ordinary men into ministry, how those who are called are a rarity, and that only those who are called by God can go for him.[34] He emphasized that an integral part of the calling was an internal desire that a person must have for ministry. In terms of Isaiah's response (and in turn the Christian minister's), Henry pointed to the prophet's readiness to go wherever God calls, his resolution to stand firm in his call, and his constant turning to God for the nature of his call. Following suit, ministers must engage in 'the work of the Lord with an entire resignation [...] to his wisdom and sovereignty. The heart must be *tabula rasa*—white paper to his pen, soft wax to his seal.'[35]

Henry then applies his exposition of this well-known passage from Isaiah 6. Atkinson was ever to remember that 'it is the work of God, Father, Son, and Spirit, to send ministers, the ambassadors of reconciliation.' Ministers must therefore regularly have their eye set upon the Triune God. In a moment of personal reflection,

---

31 Henry, *Sermon*, 968.
32 Henry, *Sermon*, 969–970.
33 Henry, *Sermon*, 970.
34 Henry, *Sermon*, 971–972.
35 Henry, *Sermon*, 973–974. The quote is from page 974.

Henry asked whether he and other seasoned ministers like him still 'had our eye up unto him [i.e. God], and a single eye; whether our desire was toward him, and our dependence upon him? Whether we took our ministry from *his* hand, and devoted it to *his* praise; I hope we did.'[36]

A central part of Henry's application of his reflections on Isaiah 6 was to note the nature of qualifications for God's call to pastoral ministry. Here, he did not focus on texts like 1 Timothy 3; rather, he continued to discuss the nature of God's equipping of the one who will be sent by him. Isaiah's attitude of 'send me' is an absolutely integral qualification for ministry. For Isaiah to ask to be sent, he was in effect asking to be 'fitted' for the work. As God's ambassadors, ministers 'never have credentials without instruction.' Like the apostles, ministers are to be sent not just with the calling of 'what to preach' but they are to be filled with 'the knowledge of the gospel mysteries.' Henry explained: 'We have nothing to give out to God's people, but what he gives in to us; nothing wherewith to fill their hearts, unless he fill our hands; as, in Ezekiel's vision, the man clothed with linen had his hands filled with coals of fire from between the cherubim.'[37] As such, preachers especially have need of the Holy Spirit's infilling 'as a spirit of revelation, that they may know the things of God; and, as a spirit of truth, to rectify their mistakes, and to lead them into all truth.'[38] They must therefore pray specifically for the Spirit's help and presence in this regard. Moreover, since ministers labour not only in speaking 'from God to his people' but also 'to God for his people', they 'have as much need of the Spirit to assist them in prayer as in preaching, and to be in them a spirit of supplication', an allusion to Zechariah 12:10. Here, in a nutshell, Henry has captured the longstanding interest that his Puritan forebears had shown in the work of the

---

36 Henry, *Sermon*, 974.

37 Henry, *Sermon*, 975.

38 Henry, *Sermon*, 975.

Holy Spirit. It is evidence of that key marker of Puritan life that Richard Lovelace has termed a 'theology of radical dependence on the Spirit',[39] and which can be abundantly found in Fuller.

Also anticipating Fuller's pastoral theology was Henry's emphasis that those who 'go for God' are not to seek their own interests and their own 'praise and applause.' As men 'entirely devoted' to God, they are to seek their Master's interests. While this should be true for all Christians, Henry was especially insistent that this must be true for pastors: 'ministers, of all people, must not live to themselves.'[40]

John Gill—'the work of a minister is [...] awful, solemn, and weighty'

The London Baptist John Gill is arguably one of the most important theologians in the denomination's history.[41] He is usually cited today for his High Calvinism that damaged far too many British Baptist communities in the eighteenth century, the extent of which is still being debated amongst historians and theologians.[42] Though definitely linked to High Calvinism, Gill should also be remembered more positively as a Reformed stalwart

---

39 Richard Lovelace, 'Pneumatological Issues in American Presbyterianism', *Greek Orthodox Theological Review*, 31 (1986): 345–346.

40 Henry, *Sermon*, 976–977.

41 John Rippon, *A Brief Memoir of the Life and Writings of the late Rev. John Gill, D.D.* (Repr. Harrisonburg, VA: Gano Books, 1992) and Michael A. G. Haykin, ed., *The Life and Thought of John Gill (1697–1771): A Tercentennial Appreciation*, Studies in the History of Christian Thought, vol.77 (Leiden: E. J. Brill, 1997) are standard introductions. See also Graham Harrison, *Dr. John Gill and His Teaching* (Annual Lecture of The Evangelical Library; London: The Evangelical Library, 1971); George M. Ella, *John Gill and the Cause of God and Truth* (Eggleston, Co. Durham: Go Publications, 1995); and Timothy George, "John Gill" in his and David S. Dockery, eds., *Theologians of the Baptist Tradition* (Rev. ed.; Nashville, TN: Broadman & Holman, 2001), 11–33.

42 See the discussion in David Mark Rathel, 'Was John Gill a Hyper-Calvinist? Determining Gill's Theological Identity', *Baptist Quarterly* 48 (2017): 47–59.

John Gill

and a theological leader whose robust Trinitarianism protected the British Baptists from the arid streams of eighteenth-century rationalism that overwhelmed other Dissenting communities, notably the Presbyterians and the General Baptists, after the Salters' Hall Synod (1719).[43] His theological acumen is evident in extensive biblical studies and a number of profound dogmatic tomes. C. H. Spurgeon captured his voluminosity when he stated, 'He was always at work; it is difficult to know when he slept, for he wrote 10,000 folio pages of theology.'[44] In fact, his early biographer John Rippon (1751–1836), a friend of Fuller, suggested that it would 'try the constitutions of half the literati in England to read, with care and attention, the whole of what he wrote.'[45] Like Henry, Gill produced a number of multi-volume commentaries on the whole of Scripture: *An Exposition of the New Testament* (3 vols.; 1746–1748), *An Exposition of the Books of the Prophets of the Old Testament* (2 vols.; 1757–1758), and *An Exposition of the Old Testament* (4 vols.; 1763–1765). As Timothy George has observed, Gill was the 'first Baptist to write a verse-by-verse commentary on the entire Bible.'[46] And his *Body of Doctrinal and Practical Divinity* was to become the standard systematic theology for many of his fellow Baptists.

Gill was born in Kettering in 1697 and as he grew up he was involved in the local Baptist church that his family helped found and where his father served as a deacon. Prior to this, his parents

---

43 See W. T. Whitley, 'Salters' Hall 1719 and the Baptists', *Transactions of the Baptist Historical Society* 5, no.3 (April 1917): 172–189.

44 C. H. Spurgeon, *Commenting on Commentaries* (London: Passmore & Alabaster, 1876), 9, quoted by Robert W. Oliver, 'John Gill (1697–1771)' in *The British Particular Baptist: 1638–1910*, ed. Michael A. G. Haykin (Springfield, MO: Particular Baptist Press, 1998), 160.

45 Rippon, *Brief Memoir*, 137.

46 Timothy George, 'John Gill' in *Theologians of the Baptist Tradition*, ed. Timothy George and David S. Dockery (Nashville, TN: Broadman & Holman Publishers, 2001), 12.

had regularly attended a Dissenting congregation that was a mixture of ecclesiological views, though they themselves held to believer's baptism. Like Matthew Henry, Gill could not attend either of the English universities, but nevertheless distinguished himself as a scholar. From a young age, he mastered 'the rudiments of Latin and Greek' and before the age of eleven had 'read through the entire Greek New Testament.'[47] As a young man, he served two area churches as an associate pastor and then in 1719 was called to a Particular Baptist church in Southwark, London. This congregation, in Horsleydown, was already an important London Baptist cause, as it had been pastored in the seventeenth century by the prolific author Benjamin Keach (1640–1704). Gill served this church for some 52 years, where his influence was also felt throughout the London Dissenting community, particularly by means of his Wednesday 'Great Eastcheap' lectures that he delivered regularly for 27 years.

As a leader amongst the London Baptists, Gill often had occasion to preach at ministerial ordinations. A small compilation of four of his ordination sermons can be found in his two-volume *A Collection of Sermons and Tracts* that was published posthumously in 1773.[48] These sermons reflect standard Evangelical approaches to pastoral theology, such as the need to maintain orthodox doctrine and sterling Christian character on the part of the minister. Here, for example, is Gill's summation of what it means to be a pastor in the sermon he preached at the ordination of John Davis (1731–1795) at Waltham Abbey on August 15, 1764:

And now, my Brother, [...] your principal work and business as a minister of the gospel [...] is to preach salvation by Christ, the doctrines of pardon by his blood, of justification by his righteousness,

---

47 James Leo Garrett Jr., *Baptist Theology: A Four-Century Study* (Macon, GA: Mercer University Press, 2009), 93.

48 John Gill, *A Collection of Sermons and Tracts: In Two Volumes* (London: George Keith, 1773), 2:1–64.

and of atonement and satisfaction for sin by his sacrifice, with other truths of the gospel; [...] you are to be laborious in this work, diligent and industrious, constant and immovable in it; [...] you are to be bold and intrepid in it, not fearing the faces of men; and to be watchful over yourself and others that are your charge; to be tender and compassionate to all in distress, whether of body, mind or estate, and to be humane in your deportment to all; [...] you are to walk uprightly, and be an example to the flock in your life and conversation; [...] you are to look up to heaven for fresh supplies of grace to carry you through your ministrations in all the branches of it; and through the whole express fervent love to Christ and the souls of men, and a zeal for his glory: and may you be a shining and burning light in your day and generation, and successful in the work of the Lord, and have many to be your joy and crown of rejoicing at the coming of Christ.[49]

Or consider the ordination sermon *The Duty of a Pastor to his People*, which Gill preached at the ordination of Oxford graduate George Braithwaite of Bridlington (1681–1748) on March 28, 1734. It was based on 1 Timothy 4:16 ('Take heed unto thyself, and unto the doctrine; continue in them: for in doing this thou shalt both save thyself, and them that hear thee'),[50] and breaks down into three parts. In the first, Gill explored how Braithwaite should 'take heed' to himself; in the second, how he should guard 'the doctrine'; and in the final section, Gill elucidated the way in which faithfulness in these two areas would issue in the salvation

---

49 John Gill, *The Doctrine of the Cherubim Opened and Explained* (*Collection of Sermons*, 2:48). Davis ministered at the Baptist church at Waltham Abbey until his death, a ministry that spanned nearly thirty years. See Geoffrey F. Nuttall, 'The Letter-Book of John Davis (1731–1795) of Waltham Abbey', *The Baptist Quarterly*, 24 (1970–1971): 58–64.

50 Gill, *The Duty of a Pastor to his People* (*Collection of Sermons*, 2:1–13), where the sermon text is listed incorrectly as 2 Timothy 4:16. For Braithwaite, see Joseph Ivimey, *History of the English Baptists* (London: Isaac Taylor Hinton and Holdsworth & Ball, 1830), 3:355–359 and Copson, 'Two Ordinations', 148, n.3.

of the pastor himself and his flock. In both halves of the sermon, Gill has a number of suggestions for each of the apostolic injunctions. For example, Braithwaite needed to make sure that he employed the gifts that God has given him as a minister and also develops them. 'Gifts, like pieces of armour', Gill observed, 'through disuse, grow rusty.' As to the ways that God has given to hone these gifts, Gill cited such means as 'prayer, meditation, and reading', which he found in the immediate context of the text of his sermon, namely, 1 Timothy 4:15.[51] The London Baptist also admonished Braithwaite to watch his time, lest he squander it through too much visitation:

> It is a mistake which prevails among church-members, that they must be visited, and that very often: if ministers are not continually calling on them they think themselves neglected, and are much displeased; not considering, that such a frequency of visits, as is desired by them, must be the bane and ruin of what might otherwise be a very valuable ministry; and at the same time furnishes an idle and lazy preacher with a good excuse to neglect his studies, and that with a great deal of peace and quietness of conscience, whilst he fancies he is about his ministerial work.[52]

Gill hastened to add that he did not think ministerial visitation overblown: it is a pastor's 'business to visit the members of the church, at proper times, and on proper occasions.' His concern was about unnecessary visits, what he termed 'the too great frequency of visits.'[53] There is obviously a tension here regarding the pastor's use of his time, which Gill has not entirely resolved by his advice to Braithwaite.

---

51 Gill, *Duty of a Pastor* (*Collection of Sermons*, 2:4–5). Like Fuller, Gill understood the reference to 'reading' in this verse to mean personal, private reading. See below, page 171.

52 Gill, *Duty of a Pastor* (*Collection of Sermons*, 2:5).

53 Gill, *Duty of a Pastor* (*Collection of Sermons*, 2:5). For Fuller's view of visitation, see below, 85, 116–116, 227–229 and 244.

Other areas in which the pastor must guard himself include being 'infected with the errors and heresies' of the day and being inwardly ruled by his passions.[54] His life also needs to be a model for other believers, where his words and behavior are in sync with one another.[55] Finally, a pastor takes heed to himself when he cares for the people in his charge, for there is 'mutual relation, a close union' between minister and pastor. Gill's words here appear to imply what is spelled out by other eighteenth-century authors, namely, that a pastor and his flock have a relationship that is akin to that between a husband and his wife.[56]

In the second half of this sermon, Gill looked at what is entailed when a pastor takes heed to his doctrine. First, his teaching must be grounded squarely on the Bible and harmonize fully with what Christ and his apostles taught. It should never advocate teachings that cannot be substantiated by Scripture.[57] It should promote holiness and never be 'subversive of true piety.'[58] And the way in which the pastor preaches must also be his concern: in preaching, a pastor is to 'speak plainly, intelligibly, and boldly.'[59]

In the final section of the sermon, Gill was at pains to point out that the Pauline admonitions to be on guard in 1 Timothy 4:16 did not mean that a pastor can literally save himself or his hearers by his ministry. What it had to mean was that a pastor will

---

54 Gill, *Duty of a Pastor* (*Collection of Sermons*, 2:6).

55 Gill, *Duty of a Pastor* (*Collection of Sermons*, 2:6–7). Here Gill cited 1 Timothy 4:12.

56 Jonathan Edwards (1703–1758), whose thought deeply influenced Fuller (see below, pages 80–82) compared the minister's relationship to the church to a marriage, a comparison that is never found in Fuller. For the comparison in Edwards, see Sean Michael Lucas, '"Divine Light. Holy Heat": Jonathan Edwards, the Ministry of the Word, and Spiritual Formation', *Presbyterion*, 34, no. 1 (Spring 2008): 3–4; Robert Caldwell, 'The Ministerial Ideal in the Ordination Sermons of Jonathan Edwards: Four Theological Points', *Themelios*, 38 (2013): 391–394.

57 Gill, *Duty of a Pastor* (*Collection of Sermons*, 2:8–10).

58 Gill, *Duty of a Pastor* (*Collection of Sermons*, 2:9)

59 Gill, *Duty of a Pastor* (*Collection of Sermons*, 2:10).

be preserved from the pollution of the world and its ideological errors. It also meant that a minister who heeds Paul's advice will be a 'means of preserving' his hearers and will be 'instrumental in their eternal salvation,' though not a cause of it.[60] As Gill noted— and this thought would be emphasized by Fuller—'the work of a minister is an awful, solemn, and weighty one.'[61]

Philip Doddridge—'equal and respectful friendship'

Philip Doddridge was a pastor, educator, author, and hymn-writer, who has become known for his moderating personality that sought to keep Nonconformity from moving to extremes.[62] Following in the footsteps of the Puritan Richard Baxter (1615–1691), who was a major influence on his thought, Doddridge hoped to develop a pan-Evangelical unity.[63] He was born in London in 1702, the twentieth child of Daniel and Monica Doddridge. His father was an oil merchant who later suffered impoverishment due to financial mismanagement. Throughout his life, the younger Doddridge was mentored by Samuel Clarke of St. Albans, whose ordination sermon was preached by Matthew Henry as discussed above. As a young man in London, he attended Clarke's Presbyterian church and eventually preached at the older man's funeral. Like Henry and Gill, Doddridge was trained at a Dissenting academy; this one in Kibworth, Leicestershire, where he later became involved

---

60 Gill, *Duty of a Pastor* (*Collection of Sermons*, 2:12–13).

61 Gill, *Duty of a Pastor* (*Collection of Sermons*, 2:12). Three years after his own ordination, George Braithwaite spoke at the ordination of Richard Machin (d.1743) and noted the 'solemnity of the church's act in her [...] constituting her pastor before God, angels, and men' (Copson, 'Two Ordinations', 147).

62 For two helpful studies of Doddridge's life and thought, see Malcolm Deacon, *Philip Doddridge of Northampton 1702–51* (Northampton: Northamptonshire Libraries, 1980) and Robert Strivens, *Philip Doddridge and the Shaping of Evangelical Dissent*, Ashgate Studies in Evangelicalism (Surrey, UK: Ashgate Publishing, 2015).

63 Alan C. Clifford, 'The Christian Mind of Philip Doddridge (1702–1751): The Gospel According to an Evangelical Congregationalist', *The Evangelical Quarterly*, 56 (1984): 228.

Philip Doddridge

in teaching. He moved to Northampton in 1729 to take the charge of the Castle Hill Independent Church and was ordained there the following year. While in Northampton, he started his own academy, based on the model he had seen at Kibworth, where he served as principal for twenty-two years. He also had a fruitful pastoral ministry, though it was cut short due to his ill health that plagued him from birth. In order to find respite and healing, Doddridge traveled to Lisbon, Portugal, but regrettably died there in 1751, where he was buried.

Like both Henry and Gill, Doddridge was also the author of a biblical commentary, *The Family Expositor* (1739–1756), though Doddridge's work was just on the New Testament.[64] Yet, his commentary, intended primarily for use in family worship, has not had the same staying power as those of his fellow Dissenters. Also like them, he was a prolific writer, and authored over fifty works, many of which were published sermons and often focused on the practicalities of the Christian life. *The Rise and Progress of Religion in the Soul* (1745), arguably his most important treatise, influenced men like Samuel Pearce (1766–1799), Fuller's close friend.[65]

Doddridge's ordination sermons can be found in a variety of sets of his works that were published after his death. In a five-volume set of Doddridge's works issued in London at the opening of the nineteenth century, there are three ordination sermons. What is most striking about the sermons is their

---

64 For a useful study of *The Family Expositor*, see Isabel Rivers, 'Philip Doddridge's New Testament: The Family Expositor (1739–56)' in Hannibal Hamlin and Norman W. Jones, *The King James Bible After Four Hundred Years: Literary, Linguistic, and Cultural Influences* (Cambridge: Cambridge University Press, 2010), 124–145.

65 Philip Doddridge, *The Rise and Progress of Religion in the Soul* (London: J. Waugh, 1745); Andrew Fuller, *Memoirs of the Rev. Samuel Pearce*, ed. Michael A.G. Haykin, The Complete Works of Andrew Fuller, vol.4 (Berlin/Boston: Walter de Gruyter, 2017), 43.

personal and warm tone in comparison with those of Henry and Gill, who are much more textual and doctrinal. Doddridge regularly addressed the candidate for ministry in affectionate terms. In fact, almost the entirety of the sermon preached at the ordination of Abraham Tozer (June 20, 1745), was framed as a series of reasons why Doddridge 'congratulates' him for his entrance into public ministry. For instance, he congratulated Tozer on 'the honour of your office', as well as the 'pleasures' of the office, and its usefulness, before turning to some warnings of the difficulties of pastoral ministry.[66] The tone throughout is familiar and encouraging.

It was in his sermon preached at the ordination of William Johnston at Wisbech on June 8, 1737, that Doddridge examined the character and qualifications of a minister of the gospel.[67] Entitled *The Temper and Conduct of the Primitive Ministers of the Gospel*, the sermon has 2 Corinthians 4:5 ('For we preach not ourselves, but Christ Jesus the Lord; and ourselves your servants for Jesus sake') for its text.[68] The sermon was structured around three basic points: first, Paul's conduct and that of his brethren in Christian ministry; second, some basic principles that can be derived from that conduct, namely the preaching of Christ; and third, some personal reflections based on the text and Doddridge's own experience. The Northampton pastor began by arguing that the apostles did not make themselves the 'chief end of their ministry', rather they were 'faithfully devoted [...] to the service of Christ.'[69] They did not seek their own applause, but because they viewed themselves as ministering in the very presence of God, their only desire was to be

---

66 Philip Doddridge, *A Charge Delivered in Norwich, at the Ordination of the Reverend Mr. Abraham Tozer; on June 20th, 1745* (*Works*, 4:253–269).

67 Philip Doddridge, *The Temper and Conduct of the Primitive Ministers of the Gospel* (*Works*, 4:210–233).

68 For Fuller's treatment of this same text in an ordination sermon, see below, pages 161–167.

69 Doddridge, *Temper and Conduct* (*Works*, 4:212).

accepted by him. Doddridge believed that this humility pervaded even Paul's writing style. Unlike the Greek orator Demosthenes, whose speeches were a model of Greek rhetoric, Paul's letters were 'written out of the fullness of his soul, but without any anxiety about style, or any very exact care even to the range of ideas according to the most methodical order.' Focused on Christ, his writing style had

> a kind of magnificent negligence. His works are a like a wilderness of beautiful and fragrant plants, spring up promiscuously out of a happy soil; and amidst all their seeming confusion, producing, to a natural taste, a finer effect than if they were drawn out with a solicitous care, set in the most regular figures, and cut into a thousand artificial forms.[70]

This lack of self-concern also meant that the apostles refused to use the ministry for financial gain or 'dominion over men's faith.'[71] Given the history of English Dissent and its persecution at the hands of the state church in the sixteenth and seventeenth centuries, it is no surprise that Doddridge emphasized the latter point. The apostles refused to extrapolate from their authority as apostles to the assumption of temporal power, which Doddridge rightly observed from the history of Christianity, has led to 'the dishonour of the Christian name, and the destruction of many.' Rather, they served their fellow believers on the basis of 'equal and respectful friendship.'[72]

The Christ-centredness of the apostles was especially manifest in their preaching. Their sermons are filled with such 'darling topics' as 'the truth of his deity, the mystery of his incarnation, the necessity of his atonement, the perfection of his righteousness,

---

70 Doddridge, *Temper and Conduct* (*Works*, 4:213–214).
71 Doddridge, *Temper and Conduct* (*Works*, 4:214–216).
72 Doddridge, *Temper and Conduct* (*Works*, 4:216, 228).

the riches of his grace.'[73] It is this apostolic concern to 'establish [Christ's] empire over the hearts and consciences of men', Doddridge averred, that must be the model for ministers of his day.[74] And just as Paul and the apostles did not simply declare these truths about Christ, but also specified how they should practically impact daily life, so ministers must insist that believers 'be careful to maintain good works' and employ their bodies and souls as 'instruments of righteousness.' Christianity, Doddridge affirmed, was not designed 'merely to amuse the world, but to reform it.'[75] Apostolic Christ-centredness was also revealed in the humility and love of Paul and his fellow apostles as they sought to serve believers, even the poorest of them. Paul, Doddridge reminded Johnston and his other hearers,

> did not disdain the meanest of the people, and was not only easy of access to them, but visited them at their own dwellings, and carried his instructions and consolations from house to house, even to those where he could expect no entertainment, but such as arose from religious converse, society in worship, and a consciousness of being useful to the souls of men.[76]

An 'affectionate love to the blessed Redeemer' was one driving force behind this preaching and ministry of Paul and the other apostles. 'A profane world censured [it] as enthusiasm and madness', but Doddridge rightly saw it as utterly foundational to the pastorate:[77]

> Was it for the sake of the Apostles alone, that the blessed Jesus stooped so low, and bore so much? Did he not love us, and give

---

73 Doddridge, *Temper and Conduct* (*Works*, 4:216–217).

74 Doddridge, *Temper and Conduct* (*Works*, 4:217).

75 Doddridge, *Temper and Conduct* (*Works*, 4:217–218).

76 Doddridge, *Temper and Conduct* (*Works*, 4:219–220).

77 Doddridge, *Temper and Conduct* (*Works*, 4:222). Here, Doddridge uses the term 'enthusiasm' with all of the negative overtones that this term bore in the eighteenth century. A modern equivalent would be 'fanaticism.'

himself for us, and was not the news of our salvation contained
in those glad tidings which he brought from heaven, which he
proclaimed on earth, publishing them with long continued labour,
and at length sealing them with his blood? [...] And where is our
gratitude, where is our fidelity, where is our common integrity, if we
can [...] lose our concern for that Gospel, in a mean solicitude about
our own applause, or interest, or dominion? I trust, my brethren, it
will never so be lost. I am persuaded, through divine grace, there are
those amongst us, whose bosoms glow with such undissembled love,
that we can truly say, we reckon the title of servants of Christ, and of
the church for his sake, a thousand times more honourable than to be
called, and to be, the lords of the whole world.[78]

Another principal motivation was 'the glory of God in the
salvation of souls.'[79] The apostles were deeply moved by the fact
that men and women, 'by sin stood exposed to everlasting darkness,
despair, and ruin', were yet living in 'a gay insensibility of danger,
and a proud confidence, on the very borders of hell.' They thus
preached 'the great doctrines of the everlasting Gospel', apart
from which nothing could 'save the perishing souls of men.'[80]
Doddridge was convinced that such a course of ministry was
not only fit for the apostolic era, but requisite for his day. As he
went on to say: 'I hope we shall never practice so dangerous a
complaisance to the unbelievers of the present age, as to wave the
Gospel, that we may accommodate ourselves to their taste; which
if we do, we may indeed preserve the name of virtue, but I fear
we shall destroy the thing itself; lose it in our congregations, and
probably in our hearts too.'[81] To bring an eternal soul to eternal
life was higher than any temporal good that could ever be done.
Having this perspective, Doddridge told Johnston, would bring

---

78 Doddridge, *Temper and Conduct* (*Works*, 4:223).
79 Doddridge, *Temper and Conduct* (*Works*, 4:224).
80 Doddridge, *Temper and Conduct* (*Works*, 4:224–225).
81 Doddridge, *Temper and Conduct* (*Works*, 4:225).

him the greatest happiness in ministry and he would be truly following in the train of the apostles, those 'blessed leaders in the army of Christ.'[82]

Conscious that he was running out of time to say much more, Doddridge offered some concluding personal reflections in the final section of this sermon. He first observed: 'How greatly is the truth of Christianity confirmed by the character of those who were first employed in the publication of it.' He was deeply thankful that the character of the apostles was recorded so that succeeding generations might have models of humility to emulate. Such emulation, Doddridge noted, can be found in

[p]ersons [...] of all denominations, both of established and separate churches, at home and abroad, who have been, and are in their respective spheres, burning and shining lights; men of God, who however different in opinion, in discipline, or in worship, have agreed to love the Lord Jesus Christ in sincerity, to bow their hearts and souls to the obedience of his laws, to value the souls committed to their care, serving them in humility and love, candidly excusing the frailties of their brethren, praying, that wherein they were otherwise minded, than reason and Scripture directed, that God would in his own time and way reveal it to them, and in the mean time labouring, that whereunto they had already attained, they might walk the same rule, and might mind the same thing.[83]

This paragraph contains, in a nutshell, Doddridge's model of catholic ministry, to which he himself aspired. He then noted the important role played by academies, like the one he ran in Northampton, in training men for pastoral ministry and how the 'sacred Scriptures are [to be] the grand magazine' in this

---

82 Doddridge, *Temper and Conduct* (*Works*, 4:226–228).
83 Doddridge, *Temper and Conduct* (*Works*, 4:230–231).

formation.[84] Doddridge closed with three quick pieces of advice to Johnston's future congregation: 'own his authority in your lives as well as your assemblies', be regular in attending worship, and not to be afraid of being transparent with him.[85]

Concluding thought

It is noteworthy that two of the sermons noted above, those of Gill and Doddridge, refer to Jesus' words about his cousin John the Baptist in John 5:35—"He was a burning and a shining light"—as a model for the Gospel minister. In his Bible commentary, Matthew Henry likewise saw this text as having application to the pastor, for

A burning light [...] denotes sincerity; painted fire may be made to shine, but that which burns is true fire. [...][Burning] denotes also [...] activity, zeal, and fervency, burning in love to God and the souls of men [...] so is a good minister.[86]

In his *Spiritual Knowledge and Love Necessary for the Ministry*, reproduced below and also based on John 5:35, Andrew Fuller encouraged the ordinand with these words: 'May you, my brother, shine in holy wisdom, and burn with ardent love.'[87] In all that Fuller will argue in his ordination sermons, this prayer forms a bedrock from which all other advice will spring. The Dissenting pastors here surveyed, and Fuller following in their train, recognised the centrality of devotion to Christ as the means by which men will be qualified for the task of pastoral ministry. The minister's calling and being equipped by God, his faithfulness in teaching sound doctrine, his living a life of personal godliness and

---

84 Doddridge, *Temper and Conduct* (*Works*, 4:231–232). The word 'magazine' here is being employed in the older meaning of a storehouse of goods.

85 Doddridge, *Temper and Conduct* (*Works*, 4:232–233).

86 Matthew Henry, *Commentary on the Whole Bible* ([Peabody, MA]: Hendrickson Publishers, 1991), 5:752.

87 Andrew Fuller, *Spiritual Knowledge and Love Necessary for the Ministry* (*Complete Works*, I, 481; see below, page 117).

pointing others to Christ—all of these aspects of biblical ministry are to be grounded in an ardent love for the Saviour. It is such a love that will help the pastor to be a burning and shining light, so that he in turn might shepherd the flock well.

Engraved by M. Branwhite.

REV. ANDREW FULLER,

Late Pastor of the Baptist Church at Kettering, and Secy to the Baptist Missionary Society. Died May 7th 1815, aged 61 Years. From the Original Painting by Medley in 1802.

Published June 19,1816, by W. Button & Son, Paternoster Row, London.

Andrew Fuller

Chapter 2: Pastoral ministry according to Andrew Fuller

The ordination sermons of Andrew Fuller constitute the largest body of such sermons by a single Baptist author in what historians term the long eighteenth century.[1] Their value as a corpus of pastoral wisdom was clearly recognized very soon after Fuller's decease in 1815 when they were published as *Hints to Ministers & Churches* in 1826. Apart from a couple of them, including a 1787 sermon discussed at length below, none of them had appeared in print prior to this point.[2] Most of them are what the 1826 collection called 'outlines', or as an anonymous reviewer put it, 'imperfect specimens of his [i.e. Fuller's] masterly style of composition' and

---

1 Keith S. Grant, *Andrew Fuller and the Evangelical Renewal of Pastoral Theology*, Studies in Baptist History and Thought, vol.36 (Milton Keynes: Paternoster, 2013), 7.

The 'long' eighteenth century is an historical moniker for the era stretching from the 1660s to the 1830s. See, for example, John Kent, 'Eighteenth century: an overview' in Adrian Hastings, *et al.* ed., *The Oxford Companion to Christian Thought* (Oxford: Oxford University Press, 2000), 195.

2 [J.G. Fuller,] 'Preface' to *Hints to Ministers & Churches* (London: B.J. Holdsworth, 1826), v.

'his very superior style of preaching.'[3] Nevertheless, they are full enough to provide a careful reader with a good understanding of what Fuller understood to be true pastoral ministry.

The pastor as 'a good man'

Now, an excellent entrée into the heart of Fuller's thoughts about the pastorate can be found in the sermon that Fuller delivered at the installation of Robert Fawkner as the pastor of Thorn Baptist Church, Bedfordshire, on October 31, 1787. Fuller preached the charge to Fawkner, which was later entitled *The Qualifications and Encouragement of a faithful Minister illustrated by the Character and Success of Barnabas*, while his close friend and first biographer John Ryland, Jr. (1753–1825) gave the charge to the Thorn congregation.[4]

This sermon has Acts 11:24 for its text, where the early Christian leader Barnabas is said to have been 'a good man, and full of the Holy Spirit, and of faith' and that as a result of his ministry 'much people was added to the Lord' in Antioch.

Fuller began by expressing his conviction that the example of

---

3 [Fuller,] 'Preface' to *Hints to Ministers & Churches*, v; 'Review: *Hints to Ministers and Churches*', *The Baptist Magazine*, 18 (1826): 420. Francis Augustus Cox (1783–1853) recalled Fuller as 'an extraordinary preacher: plain, practical, judicious, full of rich scriptural illustrations', though 'slow and solemn' in his manner of preaching (cited Joseph Belcher in Andrew Gunton Fuller, 'Memoir' in *Complete Works*, I, 105–107, note *). See also above, 25 note 14.

4 Andrew Fuller and John Ryland, *The Qualifications and Encouragement of a faithful Minister, illustrated by the Character and Success of Barnabas. And, Paul's Charge to the Corinthians respecting their Treatment of Timothy, applied to the Conduct of Churches toward Their Pastors. Being the Substance of Two Discourses, Delivered at The Settlement of The Rev. Mr. Robert Fawkner, in the Pastoral Office, Over the Baptist Church at Thorn, in Bedfordshire, October 31, 1787* (London: Thorn Baptist Church, 1787). It can be conveniently found in Fuller's *Complete Works*, I, 135–144, and below, pages 87–107.

For a discussion of this sermon, see Nigel David Wheeler, 'Eminent Spirituality and Eminent Usefulness: Andrew Fuller's (1754–1815) Pastoral Theology in his Ordination Sermons' (PhD thesis, University of Pretoria, 2009), 189–203.

other people's lives can have 'a great influence upon the human mind' for good, and especially the examples of those illustrious figures found in the Scriptures. The latter, 'drawn with the pencil of inspiration', have what Fuller called 'an assimilating tendency', that is, the record of their lives has a way of inspiring emulation and imitation. Like many in his Baptist community, Fuller deeply valued Christian biography for its instructive value.[5] As he noted in another context: 'It is good to read the lives of holy men; and the more holy they have been the better.'[6]

Fuller proceeded to examine the three characteristics mentioned in the Lukan description of Barnabas' character. First of all, Barnabas was a good man. Fuller went on to extol the importance for a pastor being marked by the virtue of goodness and noted various spheres in which goodness must be expressed. First and foremost in Fuller's mind was the pastor's own home:

> Value it [i.e. goodness] at home in your family. If you walk not closely with God there, you will be ill able to work for him elsewhere. You have lately become the head of a family. Whatever charge it shall please God, in the course of your life, to place under your care, I trust it will be your concern to recommend Christ and the gospel to them, walk circumspectly before them, constantly worship God with them, offer up secret prayer for them, and exercise a proper authority over them.[7]

The sort of instruction that Fuller gave Fawkner here regarding his behavior in his family is actually not common to ordination sermons of this era. In this case, Fuller is probably dependent on

---

5 Fuller, *Qualifications and Encouragement* (*Complete Works*, I, 135; below, page 88). See also Andrew Fuller, *On An Intimate and Practical Acquaintance with the Word of God* (*Complete Works*, I, 483; below, page 120); *idem*, *Spiritual Knowledge and Love Necessary for the Ministry* (*Complete Works*, I, 481; below, page 117).

6 Andrew Fuller, 'Memoirs of Rev. James Garie' (*Complete Works*, III, 756).

7 Fuller, *Qualifications and Encouragement* (*Complete Works*, I, 136; below, page 91).

his reading of an ordination sermon by Abraham Booth (1734–1806), whom Fuller held in very high regard.[8] Booth's *Pastoral Cautions*, preached at the ordination of Thomas Hopkins (1759–1787) in 1785, became something of a minor spiritual classic in Particular Baptist circles and was well known to Fuller.[9] In it, Booth also cautioned the new pastor about his home life:

> As it is of high importance for a young minister in single life, to behave with the utmost delicacy in all his intercourse with female friends, treating with peculiar caution those of them that are unmarried; and as it behoves him to pay the most conscientious regard to religious character, when choosing a companion for life; so, when in the conjugal state, his tenderest attention is due to the domestic happiness and the spiritual interests of his wife. This obligation, my Brother, manifestly devolves upon you; as being already a husband and a father. Next after your own soul, therefore, your wife and your children evidently claim the most affectionate, conscientious, and pious care.

> Nor can it be reasonably doubted, that many a devout and amiable woman has given her hand to a minister of the gospel, in preference to a private Christian, though otherwise equally deserving, in sanguine expectation, by so doing, of enjoying peculiar spiritual advantages in the matrimonial relation. But, alas! there is much reason to apprehend, that not a few individuals among those worthy females, have often reflected to the following effect: 'I have, indeed, married a preacher of the gospel; but I do not find in him the

---

8 'That great and good man' is the way Fuller referred to Booth in one of his ordination sermons (*Preaching Christ* [*Complete Works*, I, 501; see below, page 161]). And in 1814, Fuller noted that while Booth was alive he would refer to him as 'the first counselor' of the English Particular Baptist denomination (*Principles and Prospects of a Servant of Christ* [*Complete Works*, I, 354]).

9 See Jonathan Edwards Ryland, 'Memoir of Dr Ryland' in *Pastoral Memorials: Selected from the Manuscripts of the Late Revd. John Ryland, D.D. of Bristol* (London, 1826), I, 17.

affectionate domestic instructor, for either myself, or my children. My husband is much esteemed among his religious acquaintance, as a respectable Christian character; but his example at home is far from being delightful. Affable, condescending, and pleasing, in the parlours of religious friends; but, frequently, either trifling and unsavoury, or imperious and unsocial, in his own family. Preferring the opportunity of being entertained at a plentiful table, and of conversing with the wealthy, the polite, and the sprightly; to the homely fare of his own family, and the company of his wife and children; he often spends his afternoons and evenings from home, until so late an hour, that domestic worship is either omitted, or performed in a hasty and slovenly manner, with scarcely the appearance of devotion.—Little caring for my soul, or for the management of our growing offspring; he seems concerned for hardly anything more, than keeping fair with his people: relative to which, I have often calmly remonstrated, and submissively entreated, but all in vain. Surrounded 'with little ones, and attended with straits; destitute of the sympathies, the instructions, the consolations, which might have been expected from the affectionate heart of a pious husband, connected with the gifts of an evangelical minister; I pour out my soul to God, and mourn in secret.' Such, there is ground of apprehension, has been the sorrowful soliloquy of many a minister's pious, dutiful, and prudent wife. Take heed, then, to the best interests of your *Second-Self*.

To this end, except on extraordinary occasions, when impelled by duty, *spend your evenings at home*. Yes, and at an early hour in the evening, let your family and your study receive their demands on your presence, in the lively performance of social and secret devotion. Thus, there will be reason to hope, that domestic order and sociability, the improvement of your own understanding, and communion with God, will all be promoted.[10]

10 Abraham Booth, *Pastoral Cautions* in Michael A.G. Haykin with Alison E. Haykin, ed., *The Works of Abraham Booth* (Springfield, MO: Particular Baptist Press,

The desire to be a good man must also be seen in a pastor's public demeanour—'prove by your spirit and conduct that you are a lover of all mankind', Fuller told Fawkner. Thus, Fuller emphasized, his preaching must be grounded in a love for Jesus Christ and for the souls of those to whom he preached. As Fuller warned Fawkner: 'Hundreds of ministers have been ruined by indulging a thirst for the character of the *great* man, while they have neglected the far superior character of the *good* man.' The pursuit of personal goodness must ever be a priority of the pastor's life.[11]

'Learn your religion from the Bible'

But how is such goodness to be obtained? Alluding to another passage from Acts, namely, Acts 6:4, Fuller emphasized two key means of spiritual formation and spiritual vitality: Fawkner was to be devoted to personal study of 'the Word of God, and to prayer.'[12] Right from the very beginning of his own ministry, Fuller had sought to build his life and thought on the Word of God. As he said in the first draft (1778) of *The Gospel Worthy of All Acceptation*: 'O Lord, impress thy Truth upon my heart with thine own seal.'[13] Fuller was an ardent reader of the Scriptures for he regarded them as 'the book by way of eminence, the book of books.'[14] The Scriptures occupied such a place of pre-eminence in his

---

2006), 1:66–67.

11 Fuller, *Qualifications and Encouragement* (*Complete Works*, I, 137–138; below, pages 93–94).

12 In his funeral sermon for his friend John Sutcliff, Fuller made the point that it is 'by a growing acquaintance with the word of God, accompanied with habitual prayer, that the love of God increases and abounds more and more' (*Principles and Prospects* [*Complete Works*, I, 345]). See also Andrew Fuller, *Ministers Fellow Labourers with God* (*Complete Works*, I, 492; below, pages 139–140).

13 Andrew Fuller, 'Thoughts on the Power of Men to Do the Will of God' (Ms., 1777/1778; Archives, James P. Boyce Centennial Library, The Southern Baptist Theological Seminary), 1.

14 Andrew Fuller, 'The Apostolic Office' (*Complete Works*, III, 498–499).

mind because, unlike all other books, they are 'unerring'[15] and are characterized by 'Divine inspiration and infallibility.'[16] As Fuller stated in another sermon:

Many religious people appear to be contented with seeing truth in the light in which some great and good man has placed it; but if ever we enter into the gospel to purpose, it must be by reading the word of God for ourselves, and by praying and meditating upon its sacred contents. It is 'in God's light that we must see light' [cf. Psalm 36:9] [...] The writings of great and good men are not to be despised, any more than their preaching: only let them not be treated as oracular. The best of men, in this imperfect state, view things *partially*, and therefore are in danger of laying an improper stress upon some parts of Scripture, to the neglect of other parts of equal, and sometimes of superior importance. [...] If we adopt the principles of fallible men, without searching the Scriptures for ourselves, and inquiring whether or not these things be so, they will not, even allowing them to be on the side of truth, avail us, as if we had learned them from a higher authority. Our faith, in this case, will stand in the wisdom of man, and not in the power of God. [...] Truth learned only at second-hand will be to us what Saul's armour was to David; we shall be at a loss how to use it in the day of trial.[17]

Here, Fuller differentiated between the books of fallible men, albeit good thinkers, and the truth of God in Scripture. The writings of fallible men are, at best, unable to provide the nourishment necessary for genuine spiritual growth. And because they stem from fallible minds, they are inevitably partial perspectives on the truth and inadequate to support either the believer or the pastor in times of trial. By contrast, Scripture is a

---

15 Andrew Fuller, *On Spiritual Declension and the Means of Revival* (*Complete Works*, III, 629).

16 Andrew Fuller, *The Nature and Importance of an Intimate Knowledge of Divine Truth* (*Complete Works*, I, 160).

17 Fuller, *Intimate Knowledge of Divine Truth* (*Complete Works*, I, 164).

sure guide for both pastor and believer, for it brings godly balance and perspective to their lives and provides them with a wholly adequate support in the face of life's challenges.

Fuller made essentially the same point in another sermon, which was based on Ezra 7:10 and was preached in August of 1787 at the ordination of John West to the pastorate of the Baptist cause in Carlton, Bedfordshire—thus, but a few months before Fuller's Thorn sermon. Fuller urged West:

> Learn your religion from the Bible. Let that be your decisive rule. Adopt not a body of sentiments, or even a single sentiment, solely on the authority of any man—however great, however respected. Dare to think for yourself. Human compositions are fallible. But the Scriptures were written by men who wrote as they were inspired by the Holy Spirit.[18]

Fuller was also adamant that pastors must live by the truth of Scripture. Reflecting upon Paul's admonition at the close of his first letter to Timothy to hold fast the gospel and truth (1 Timothy 6:20), Fuller asserted:

> The best way to hold fast the truth as a minister is to live upon it as a Christian. Attempt to keep it anywhere but in your heart, and it will go. [...] It is living upon the truth as a Christian that will cause the heart to be established with grace.[19]

Fuller never forgot that faithful pastors are Christians first, and must nourish their own souls if they were to nourish others with

---

18 Fuller, *Intimate and Practical Acquaintance* (*Complete Works*, I, 483; below, page 121). See also Fuller, *Spiritual Knowledge and Love Necessary* (*Complete Works*, I, 481–482; below, pages 117–117); *idem, Habitual Devotedness to the Ministry* (*Complete Works*, I, 507; below, page 173).

On West, see Michael A.G. Haykin, ed., *The Armies of the Lamb: The spirituality of Andrew Fuller* (Dundas, ON: Joshua Press, 2001), 114, n.2.

19 Andrew Fuller, *The Work and Encouragements of the Christian Minister* (*Complete Works*, I, 498; below, page 153).

the gospel. As Fuller put it in a Puritan-like pithy saying: 'Take refuge in the Saviour you recommend to others.'[20] And as he warned the theological students at Stepney Academical Institution in London: 'Tremble at the idea of being a graceless minister.'[21]

'Habitual dealing with Christ'

Also significant in the sermon at Robert Fawkner's ordination were Fuller's remarks about prayer:

> Beware also, brother, of neglecting secret prayer. The fire of devotion will go out if it be not kept alive by an habitual dealing with Christ. Conversing with men and things may brighten our gifts and parts; but it is conversing with God that must brighten our graces. Whatever ardour we may feel in our public work, if this is wanting, things cannot be right, nor can they in such a train come to a good issue.[22]

'The fire of devotion', as Fuller put it, was utterly vital for pastoral ministry. And such devotion needed the fuel of prayer to keep it bright and enflamed. As noted above, Fuller is usually remembered today for either his activism in the genesis of the modern missionary movement or his acumen as an apologist for the Christian Faith.[23] But informing both his activism and his apologetics was a recognition that prayer had to be a priority in his

---

20 Andrew Fuller, *Habitual Devotedness to the Ministry* (*Complete Works*, I, 508; below, page 175).

21 Andrew Fuller, *The Young Minister Exhorted to Make Full Proof of His Ministry* (*Complete Works*, I, 520; below, page 191).

22 Fuller, *Qualifications and Encouragement* (*Complete Works*, I, 137; below, page 92).

23 Both of these marks of Fuller's character and ministry were noticed during his lifetime. In an obituary at the time of his death in 1815, the question was asked: 'for clearness of conception, for strength and vigour of mind, for decision of character, for laborious exertion, for punctuality and promptness in all his measure, where shall we find his equal?' ('Obituary', *The New Evangelical Magazine and Theological Review*, 1 [1815]: 192).

own life and ministry if he were ever going to be useful for God. As Peter Morden, the author of an excellent biography of Fuller, has noted with regard to Fuller: 'He was most effective as a man of action when he was first and foremost a man of prayer.'[24] Thus Fuller stressed in the charge given to John West:

Let all your private meditations [on the Bible] be mingled with prayer. You will study your Bible to wonderful advantage, if you go to it spiritually-minded. It is this which causes us to see the beauty and to feel the force of many parts of Scripture.[25]

John Sutcliff

Again, as Fuller noted in another ordination sermon, this one from John 5:35, 'Walking with God in the closet is a grand means, with his blessing, of illuminating our minds and warming our hearts.'[26] And in one of Fuller's final sermons, preached at the funeral of his close friend, John Sutcliff (1752–1814) of Olney, Buckinghamshire, Fuller hammered home the same point: 'There is no intercourse with God without prayer. It is thus that we walk with God.'[27] As Fuller

---

24 'Feel like you're neglecting your own spiritual life? Find out why Spurgeon's College has opened a Centre for Spirituality', *Baptist Times*, 12/06/2015 (https://www.baptist.org.uk/Articles/441526/Neglecting_your_own.aspx; accessed March 7, 2019).

25 Fuller, *Intimate and Practical Acquaintance* (*Complete Works*, I, 484; below, page 123).

26 Andrew Fuller, *Spiritual Knowledge and Love Necessary* (*Complete Works*, I, 482; below, page 118).

27 Fuller, *Principles and Prospects* (*Complete Works*, I, 344). See also his 'Sermon on the Mount: Alms-giving, and Prayer' (*Complete Works*, I, 576): 'It is taken for granted

once summed up this point: 'Personal religion is of the utmost importance to a minister.'[28]

'Full of the Holy Spirit and of faith'

Barnabas was also a man, according to Luke's description of him in Acts 11, who was 'full of the Holy Spirit', which Fuller understood to mean that Barnabas was full of the fruit of the Spirit mentioned in Galatians 5:22–23. In his words:

> To be full of the Holy Spirit is to be full of the dove, as I may say; or full of those fruits of the Spirit mentioned by the apostle to the Galatians; namely, 'love, joy, peace, long-suffering, gentleness, goodness.' [...] A person that is greatly under the influence of the love of this world is said to be drunken with its cares or pleasures. In allusion to something like this, the apostle exhorts that we 'be not drunken with wine, wherein is excess; but filled with the Spirit' [Ephesians 5:18]. The word 'filled', here, is very expressive; it denotes, I apprehend, being overcome, as it were, with the holy influences and fruits of the blessed Spirit. How necessary is all this, my brother, in your work! Oh how necessary is 'an unction from the Holy One' [1 John 2:20]![29]

Fuller's interpretation here of the term 'unction' from 1 John 2:20 was taken directly from John Gill. In his own commentary on this

---

that Christ's disciples are praying men [...] Christians cannot live without communion with God'; *idem, Causes of Declension in Religion, and Means of Revival* (*Complete Works*, III, 324): 'Finally, brethren, let us not forget to intermingle prayer with all we do. Our need of God's Holy Spirit to enable us to do any thing, and everything, truly good, should excite us to do this. [...] Constantly and earnestly, therefore, let us approach his throne. Take all occasions especially for closet prayer. Here, if anywhere, we shall get fresh strength, and maintain a life of communion with God.'

28 Andrew Fuller, *Ministers Appointed to Root Out Evil, and to Cultivate Good* (*Complete Works*, I, 488; below, page 132). The authors are indebted to Jeremy Walker, '"On the Side of God": Andrew Fuller's Pastoral Theology" in *The Power of God* ([London]: Westminster Conference, 2015), 12, for this quote.

29 Fuller, *Qualifications and Encouragement* (*Complete Works*, I, 138, 139; below, page 95).

passage, Gill had delineated that the 'unction' or 'anointing' that believers received from the Holy One, that is, the Lord Jesus, was the 'Spirit, and his graces.'[30]

In Fuller's mind, there were five ways in which this unction from the Spirit shapes a pastor's life. First of all, it enabled the pastor 'to enter into the spirit of the gospel' and to rightly understand the truths at the heart of the Christian Faith. In fact, Fuller was convinced that if Christians in general 'had more of the Holy Spirit of God in their hearts', there would be far less friction between them concerning such great truths as 'the loveliness of the divine character', 'the exceeding sinfulness of sin, the total depravity of mankind, the proper deity and atonement of Christ, justification by faith in his name, the freeness and sovereignty of grace, and the agency of the Holy Spirit.'[31] All of these truths had come into dispute in eighteenth-century England as a result of the rationalism of the British Enlightenment and, Fuller implied, only the Holy Spirit's presence could protect the pastor against speculations aroused by this corrosive rationalism.[32] Little wonder he urged Fawkner to make Psalm 51:11 his prayer: 'Take not thy Holy Spirit from me.'[33]

Second, Fuller was convinced that 'being full of the Holy Spirit' will lead a preacher to use the very words of Holy Scripture that the Holy Spirit has inspired rather than various alternatives which, while they might be more familiar to the ears of the preacher's audience, nonetheless subtly change the meaning of what is being

---

30 John Gill, *An Exposition of the New Testament* (Rev. ed.; London: George Keith, 1776), 5:355–356.

31 Fuller, *Qualifications and Encouragement* (*Complete Works*, I, 139; below, page 96).

32 See also Andrew Fuller, *Churches Walking in the Truth, the Joy of Ministers* (*Complete Works*, I, 530); idem, *Faith in the Gospel a Necessary Prerequisite to Preaching It* (*Complete Works*, I, 516; below, pages 182–182). This latter address was preached to the students at Bristol Baptist Academy.

33 Fuller, *Qualifications and Encouragement* (*Complete Works*, I, 139; below, page 97).

communicated. Examples of such sermonic substitutions from his own day, according to Fuller, were to use 'morality' in place of 'holiness', 'virtue' instead of 'godliness', 'good men' for 'believers [and] saints', or to replace 'communion with God' with 'happiness of mind.' If such substitutions become the norm, Fuller reasoned, it will result in 'the gospel heathenized, and will tend to heathenize the minds' of both the preacher and hearer. For Fuller, the Spirit's help is not only vital in the discernment of biblical truth, but also in its communication: 'spiritual things will be spiritually discerned, and if spiritually discerned, will be spiritually communicated.' The anointing of the Holy Spirit will thus give a man a desire to speak in the very language used by the Holy Spirit in the Scriptures. As Fuller told Fawkner: the more you are filled with 'an unction from the Holy One, the greater relish you will possess for that savoury manner of conveying truth' as found in terms drawn directly from the Bible.[34] Fuller's use of affective terms here—'relish' and 'savoury'—is noteworthy. It is obvious that, for Fuller, the infilling of the Holy Spirit is closely tied to the creation of a spiritual appetite.

Then, the Spirit's anointing will be seen in a harmony between what a man preaches and inculcates from the pulpit and how he lives his life, for, and here Fuller cited Proverbs 17:7 as proof, 'Excellent speech becometh not a fool.'[35] Fourth, this anointing will 'give a spiritual savour' to the minister's speech as he visits the members of his church and enables him to love them.[36] Finally, the

---

34 Fuller, *Qualifications and Encouragement* (*Complete Works*, I, 140; below, pages 98–99). See also Fuller, *Intimate and Practical Acquaintance* (*Complete Works*, I, 484; below, pages 120–122); *idem, The Satisfaction Derived from Godly Simplicity* (*Complete Works*, I, 540–541); *idem, Strictures on Some of the Leading Sentiments of Mr. R. Robinson* (*Complete Works*, III, 609): 'I must confess, I am [...] attached to Scripture phraseology.'

35 Fuller, *Qualifications and Encouragement* (*Complete Works*, I, 140; below, page 99).

36 Fuller, *Qualifications and Encouragement* (*Complete Works*, I, 140–141; below, pages 99–100).

Spirit's infilling will impart to the minister 'a meek, mild, peaceful, humble spirit.' It is noteworthy that these final three effects of the Spirit's anointing concern more than simply the act of sermon preparation and its delivery. The unction of the Spirit, in Fuller's thinking, does not simply relate to empowerment in preaching, but has an effect upon the whole of the preacher's life and ministry.

The final, and third, characteristic of Barnabas' life was that he was full of faith. Fuller took this to be expressive of three ideas. Barnabas had a mind 'stored with divine sentiment', that is, he had deep personal convictions about the vital truths of the Bible. Then, he was 'rooted and grounded in the truth of the gospel.' Third, his was a life that daily fed upon the gospel.[37]

'Eminent usefulness'

Fuller's spirituality was very much that of an activist. After the formation of the Baptist Missionary Society in October of 1793, Fuller became the first secretary of the society until his death in 1815. The work of the mission consumed an enormous amount of Fuller's time as he regularly toured the country, representing the mission and raising funds. On average he was away from home three months of the year. Between 1798 and 1813, for instance, he made five lengthy and arduous trips to Scotland for the mission as well as undertaking journeys to Wales and Ireland.[38] For example, on one of these trips, that made to Scotland in 1805, Fuller travelled thirteen hundred miles and preached fifty sermons in around sixty days. As the mission secretary he also carried on an extensive correspondence both to the missionaries on the field and

---

37 Fuller, *Qualifications and Encouragement* (*Complete Works*, I, 141–142; below, pages 100–103).

38 On Fuller's trips to Scotland, see Dudley Reeves, 'Andrew Fuller in Scotland', *The Banner of Truth*, 106–107 (July/August 1972): 33–40; Michael A.G. Haykin, 'Andrew Fuller and his Scottish friends', *History Scotland*, 15, no.6 (November/ December 2015): 24–30.

to supporters at home. And finally, he had supervise the selection of missionary appointees and sought to deal with troubles as they emerged on the field. In short, he acted as the pastor of the missionaries sent out.[39] The amount of energy and time this took deeply worried his friends. As one of his friends, Robert Hall, Jr. (1764–1831), put it in a letter to John Ryland: 'if he [i.e. Fuller] is not more careful he will be in danger of wearing himself out before his time. His journeys, his studies, his correspondcies [*sic*] must be too much for the constitution of any man.'[40]

It is not surprising, therefore, that Fuller concluded his sermon for Fawkner with a reference to serving Christ and his kingdom. As he put it, 'eminent spirituality in a minister is usually attended with eminent usefulness', where 'eminent spirituality' is to be understood in light of what Fuller has already said about the fullness of the Holy Spirit/the Holy Spirit's anointing.[41] Fuller stressed that this affirmation was not meant to imply that piety automatically guaranteed success:

> I do not mean to say our usefulness depends upon our spirituality, as an effect depends upon its cause; nor yet that it is always in proportion to it. God is a Sovereign; and frequently sees proper to convince us of it, in variously bestowing his blessing on the means of grace.[42]

In other words, he was convinced as was most of western

---

39 Doyle L. Young, 'Andrew Fuller and the Modern Mission Movement', *Baptist History and Heritage*, 17 (1982): 17–27.

40 Letter to John Ryland, Jr., May 25, 1801, cited Geoffrey F. Nuttall, 'Letters from Robert Hall to John Ryland 1791–1824', *The Baptist Quarterly* 34 (1991–1992): 127.

41 Fuller, *Qualifications and Encouragement* (*Complete Works*, I, 143; below, page 104). See also Andrew Fuller, *Affectionate Concern of a Minister for the Salvation of his Hearers* (*Complete Works*, I, 508; below, page 176).

42 Fuller, *Qualifications and Encouragement* (*Complete Works*, I, 143; below, page 104). See also Fuller, *Habitual Devotedness to the Ministry* (*Complete Works*, I, 508; below, page 174); Wheeler, 'Eminent Spirituality and Eminent Usefulness', 202.

Christianity after the fourth-century Donatist controversy that 'the quality and state of he who administers the sacraments and the Word of God [...] did not have an influence on its efficacy.'[43] On the other hand, Fuller was certain that 'our want of usefulness is often to be ascribed to our want of spirituality, much oftener than to our want of talents.' Men, who seemed destined to be greatly used by God because of their gifts, have turned out otherwise and that because their inner lives were marred by 'such things as pride, unwatchfulness, carnality, and levity.'[44]

Why did Fuller hold that usefulness in God's service cannot be divorced from spirituality or what he called 'eminency in grace'? First, he argued that where there is true spirituality, the soul burns 'with holy love to Christ and the souls of men.' It gives the possessor an unquenchable passion to see God and Christ glorified and men and women converted. Fuller pointed to a number of men who were great examples in this regard: Old Testament saints like Hezekiah, Ezra and Nehemiah and various figures in the history of the Church, men such as Peter and Paul, John Wycliffe, Martin Luther and John Calvin, as well as '[John] Elliot [*sic*], and [Jonathan] Edwards, and [David] Brainerd, and [George] Whitefield.'[45] It is noteworthy that in the group of Christian worthies from the seventeenth and eighteenth centuries, three of them—Eliot, Brainerd, and Whitefield—were admired in Fuller's day for their activism, in a word, their ceaseless missionary endeavours to reach the lost with the gospel. The fourth figure, Edwards—rightly described by Miklós Vetö as 'the greatest

---

43 Alexander Bitzel, 'The Theology of the Sermon in the Eighteenth Century', trans. Charlotte Masemann in *Preaching, Sermon and Cultural Change in the Long Eighteenth Century*, ed. Joris van Eijnatten (Leiden/Boston: Brill, 2009), 64.

44 Fuller, *Qualifications and Encouragement* (*Complete Works*, I, 143; below, page 104).

45 Fuller, *Qualifications and Encouragement* (*Complete Works*, I, 143; below, page 106).

Jonathan Edwards

Christian theologian of the eighteenth century'[46]—was Fuller's main theological and spiritual guide after the Scriptures.[47] This list also reflects Fuller's catholicity and willingness to look beyond his own Particular Baptist heritage for models in ministry. And yet it bears noting that, after the death of his close friend Samuel Pearce (1766–1799) of Birmingham, Fuller did not hesitate to recommend this Baptist pastor as a model preacher. As he stated in a later ordination sermon with regard to the way in which the gospel should be preached:

> Consider the examples held up for your imitation. You have Peter [...] Paul [...] John [...] Nay, more—you have Christ. Nor have you examples in distant ages only; but you have seen some, even among you [...] Pearce![48]

'Eminent spirituality' also produces an ardency for 'the glory of God, and the welfare of men's souls', which are 'ends which God himself pursues.' Thus, one can hope for God's 'blessing to attend our labours.' As Fuller pithily observed in another ordination sermon, 'a cold manner' in preaching 'disgraces important truth.'[49]

---

46 Miklós Vetö, 'Book Reviews: *America's Theologian: A Recommendation of Jonathan Edwards*. By Robert W. Jenson', *Church History*, 58 (1989): 522.

47 For the influence of Edwards on Fuller, see especially Chris Chun, *The Legacy of Jonathan Edwards in the Theology of Andrew Fuller*, Studies in the History of Christian Traditions, vol. 162 (Leiden/Boston: Brill, 2012).

48 Fuller, *The Nature of the Gospel, and Manner in Which It Ought to Be Preached* (*Complete Works*, I, 496; below, pages 149–150). See also his *Spiritual Knowledge and Love Necessary* (*Complete Works*, I, 481; below, page 117); *idem, Affectionate Concern of a Minister* (*Complete Works*, I, 508; below, page 177): 'Look at the men who have been the most honoured; and you will find that they are not the brightest geniuses, but the humble and affectionate.'

For Fuller's biographical study of Pearce, see his *Memoirs of the Rev. Samuel Pearce, M.A.* (*Complete Works*, III, 367–446). See also Michael A. G. Haykin, *Joy unspeakable and full of glory: The piety of Samuel and Sarah Pearce* (Kitchener, ON: Joshua Press, 2012); *idem*, ed., *Memoirs of the Rev. Samuel Pearce*, The Complete Works of Andrew Fuller, vol. 4 (Berlin/Boston: Walter de Gruyter, 2017).

49 Fuller, *Affectionate Concern of a Minister* (*Complete Works*, I, 510; below, page 180).

Finally, Fuller believed that a person who is marked by 'eminency in grace' will also be a person of genuine humility and it is safe for him 'to be much owned of God.' Success will not go to his head.[50] In fact, Fuller wondered if 'one considerable reason why most of us have no more real success in our work than we have' is because 'we have not grace enough to bear prosperity.'[51]

'The sweetest of all sweets'

In his Thorn sermon, Fuller did not flesh out in greater detail his assertion here that one of the key fruits of 'eminent spirituality' in the life of a pastor is love. Elsewhere, though, he usually encouraged pastors to exercise a ministry marked by love above all things, for the 'gospel is a message of love, and therefore it ought to be preached with great affection.'[52] For instance, in June of 1802, he told the Cannon Street congregation assembled in Birmingham for the ordination of Thomas Morgan (1776–1857): 'Love is the grand secret to make you all happy' as pastor and people.[53] Yet again, Fuller told a congregation, the only true bond to bind together pastor and people was 'love'.[54] And Fuller made the same point in a sermon entitled *Moses' Choice*, where he declared regarding love:

> The society of the people of God, though afflicted, reproached, and persecuted, exceeds all the pleasures of sin, while they last. It is delightful to cast in our lot with them; for the bond of their union

---

50 Fuller, *Qualifications and Encouragement* (*Complete Works*, I, 144; below, pages 106–107).

51 Fuller, *Qualifications and Encouragement* (*Complete Works*, I, 144; below, page 107).

52 Fuller, *Nature of the Gospel* (*Complete Works*, I, 496; below, page 149).

53 Andrew Fuller, *The Obedience of Churches to their Pastors Explained and Enforced* (*Complete Works*, I, 202). See also Fuller, *Work and Encouragements* (*Complete Works*, I, 499; below, page 155).

54 Andrew Fuller, *Churches Walking in the Truth the Joy of Ministers* (*Complete Works*, I, 530).

is holy love, which is the sweetest of all sweets to a holy mind. If we have once tasted of this, everything else will become comparatively insipid. How sweet a bond is the love of Christ—how sweet is the fellowship of the saints![55]

Moreover, love was essential, Fuller argued, when it came to pastoral leadership: 'The great art of presiding in a church, so as to promote its welfare, is to be neutral between the members, always on the side of God and righteousness, and to let them see that, whatever your opinion may be, you really love them.'[56] And in an ordination sermon based on an exposition of John 5:35 ('He was a burning and shining light'), Fuller noted that in this text, spoken initially by the Lord Jesus about his cousin, John the Baptist, Jesus was commending 'spiritual light and holy love' as marks of a true gospel ministry.[57] It is vital to note that Fuller did not see the pastor's insistence on biblical doctrine as a contradiction of his emphasis that pastoral ministry must be conducted in an atmosphere of love. In fact, Fuller argued at one point that to be a faithful pastor is to 'root out errors in doctrine' with 'the pure love' of one who has been appointed to preserve his people 'from things

55 Andrew Fuller, *Moses' Choice* in *Miscellaneous Pieces on Various Religious Subjects, Being the Last Remains of the Rev. Andrew Fuller*, collected and arranged J.W. Morris (London: Wightman and Cramp, 1826), 296.

56 Fuller, *Spiritual Knowledge and Love Necessary* (*Complete Works*, I, 481; below, page 115). See also Andrew Fuller, *Pastors Required to Feed the Flock of Christ* (*Complete Works*, I, 477–478; below, page 109); *idem*, *Affectionate Concern of a Minister* (*Complete Works*, I, 508–510; below, pages 176–180); *idem*, *Nature and Importance of Christian Love* (*Complete Works*, I, 522–524); *idem*, *Ministers and Churches Exhorted to Serve One Another in Love* (*Complete Works*, I, 544–545; below, pages 196–198). For love as a bond between pastor and people, see Grant, *Andrew Fuller and the Evangelical Renewal of Pastoral Theology*, 67–68; Walker, 'On the Side of God', 17–19, and especially Paul A. Sanchez, *The Spirituality of Love in Andrew Fuller's Ordination Sermons* (Louisville, KY: The Andrew Fuller Center for Baptist Studies, 2018).

57 Fuller, *Spiritual Knowledge and Love Necessary* (*Complete Works*, I, 478–479; below, pages 111–111). It is noteworthy that Fuller could remark in another sermon that the 'truth is a system of love and goodness' (*Churches Walking in the Truth* [*Complete Works*, I, 529]).

that tend to the ruin of their souls.'[58] It is only by such love that a pastor can speak the truth, both publicly and privately.[59]

Fuller's view of love as the heart of congregational life together also meant that he abhorred the abuse of pastoral authority, what he called some pastors' 'fondness for power, aspiring to the exercise of dominion over their brethren.' Such men speak and act as 'if churches were made for them, rather than they for churches.'[60] They love being admired, regard themselves 'person[s] of consequence', and consider it 'a fine thing' if they 'have a black coat', which was a distinguishing mark of many ministers in eighteenth-century England.[61] As a partial remedy, Fuller urged pastors to remember the meaning of the word 'minister': it denotes a 'servant'. Pastors are thus called by God to serve for the well-being of God's people and to enable them to flourish.[62]

'Shame covers my face'

Fuller's sermon was so well received that the Church at Thorn

58 Fuller, *Ministers Appointed to Root Out Evil* (*Complete Works*, I, 487; below, page 129).

59 Fuller, *Ministers Fellow Labourers* (*Complete Works*, I, 492–493; below, page 141). Fuller was convinced that a 'considerable part of the pastoral office consists in visiting the people' (*Spiritual Knowledge and Love Necessary* [*Complete Works*, I, 481; below, page 115]). See also his *Obedience of Churches* (*Complete Works*, I, 198, 199); idem, *Intimate and Practical Acquaintance* (*Complete Works*, I, 486; below, page 126); idem, *Ministers Appointed to Root Out Evil* (*Complete Works*, I, 487; below, page 130); idem, *Ministers Should Be Concerned Not to Be Despised* (*Complete Works*, I, 490; below, page 136); idem, *Ministers Fellow Labourers* (*Complete Works*, I, 492–493; below, page 141); idem, *The Influence of the Presence of Christ on a Minister* (*Complete Works*, I, 505; below, page 170).

60 Fuller, *Young Minister Exhorted* (*Complete Works*, I, 519; below, page 188);

61 Fuller, *Ministers and Churches Exhorted* (*Complete Works*, I, 544; below, pages 196–199). Since the Reformation, many ministers in the Protestant tradition had worn black clothing.

62 Fuller, *Ministers and Churches Exhorted* (*Complete Works*, I, 544; below, pages 196–198); idem, *Young Minister Exhorted* (*Complete Works*, I, 518–519; below, pages 188–189).

urged its publication along with one given by John Ryland. The following summer, in July of 1788, Fuller wrote to Benjamin Francis (1734–1799), the pastor of a Particular Baptist congregation in Horsley, Gloucestershire, and mentioned that his Thorn sermon had been published. Recalling what he had preached, though, caused Fuller to reflect on the way in which he personally fell short of living according to what he had said on that October day in Thorn:

> My greatest difficulties arise from within. I am not what a servant of Christ should be. I want an unction from the Holy One. I have lately preached an ordination sermon or two, (that at Thorn, which is printed, for one[63]) in which I have endeavoured to come as home to the heart and conscience of my brethren as I knew how. But, oh, what shame covers my face when I turn my attention inward! I am the man who am too, too guilty of many of those things which I have cautioned them to avoid.[64]

The clause 'unction from the Holy One' is, of course, a reference to 1 John 2:20, which, as has been noted above, Fuller understood to be a reference to the Holy Spirit. By lamenting his own perceived lack of such a fullness of the Spirit, Fuller was obviously indicating his ardency for and prizing of such a blessing. Without such an unction, or fullness of the Spirit, he knew that he could not be a useful servant of Christ, for, as he had put it in his Thorn sermon, 'eminent spirituality in a minister is usually attended with eminent usefulness.'[65]

---

63 The other sermon was the sermon for John West—*Intimate and Practical Acquaintance* (*Complete Works*, I, 483–486; below, pages 120–127), as noted above.

64 Andrew Fuller, Letter to Benjamin Francis, July 13, 1788, in *The Baptist Magazine* 34 (1842): 637–638. This letter is also reprinted in Haykin, ed., *Armies of the Lamb*, 111–113.

65 Fuller, *Qualifications and Encouragement* (*Complete Works*, I, 143; below, page 104).

Part II: The ordination sermons of Andrew Fuller

1. The Qualifications and Encouragement of a Faithful Minister Illustrated by the Character and Success of Barnabas[1]

'He was a good man, and full of the Holy Spirit, and of faith; and much people was added to the Lord' (Acts 11:24).

My dear brother:

---

1 *Complete Works*, I, 135–144. This sermon was preached at the ordination of Robert Fawkner at Thorn, Bedfordshire, October 31, 1787. The Thorn Baptist Church is now known as Houghton Regis Baptist Church. The roots of this church go back to the 1670s and 1680s when a group of men and women were led by Thomas Hayward (d.1688) who has been described as 'simply a man called to lead people who wished to worship in their own way, without using the Book of Common Prayer' of the state church. The Thorn Church, though, was not formally constituted till 1751. The first minister was Thomas Bunker (d.1769). After becoming the pastor, Fawkner began services also in his home in Houghton Regis, which would be the origin of the Houghton Regis congregation. For a while, it was a two-point charge, but in the nineteenth century, the members of the two congregations were merged into one church at Houghton Regis. The Thorn building in which Fuller preached was demolished and the bricks taken to Houghton Regis to help enlarge the church building there. See 'HRBC Church history', *Houghton Regis Baptist Church* (http://houghtonregisbaptistchurch.blogspot.com/p/hrbc-church-history.html; accessed March 24, 2019).

It is a very important work to which you are this day set apart. I feel the difficulty of your situation. You need both counsel and encouragement; I wish I were better able to administer both. In what I may offer, I am persuaded you will allow me to be free; and understand me, not as assuming any authority or superiority over you, but only as saying that to you which I wish to consider as equally addressed to myself.

Out of a variety of topics that might afford a lesson for a Christian minister, my thoughts have turned, on this occasion, upon that of example. Example has a great influence upon the human mind: examples from Scripture especially, wherein characters the most illustrious in their day, for gifts, grace, and usefulness, are drawn with the pencil of inspiration, have an assimilating tendency. Viewing these, under a divine blessing, we form some just conceptions of the nature and importance of our work, are led to reflect upon our own defects, and feel the fire of holy emulation kindling in our bosoms.

The particular example, my brother, which I wish to recommend to your attention is that of Barnabas, that excellent servant of Christ and companion of the apostle Paul. You will find his character particularly given in the words I have just read.

Were we to examine the life of this great and good man, as related in other parts of Scripture, we should find the character here given him abundantly confirmed. He seems to have been one of that great company who, through the preaching of Peter and the other apostles, submitted to Christ soon after his ascension; and he gave early proof of his love to him, by selling his possessions, and laying the price at the feet of the apostles for the support of his infant cause. As he loved Christ, so he loved his people. He

For its publication data, see above page 66, note 4, It can also be found in Keith S. Grant, *Andrew Fuller and the Evangelical Renewal of Pastoral Theology*, Studies in Baptist History and Thought, vol.36 (Milton Keynes: Paternoster, 2013), 112–125.

appears to have possessed much of the tender and affectionate, on account of which he was called 'Barnabas—a son of consolation.' Assiduous in discovering and encouraging the first dawnings of God's work, he was the first person that introduced Saul into the company of the disciples. The next news that we hear of him is in the passage which I have selected. Tidings came to the ears of the church at Jerusalem of the Word of the Lord being prosperous at Antioch, in Syria. The church at Jerusalem was the mother church, and felt a concern for others, like that of a tender mother towards her infant offspring. The young converts at Antioch wanted a nursing father; and who so proper to be sent as Barnabas? He goes; and, far from envying the success of others, who had laboured before him, he 'was glad to see the grace of God' so evidently appear; 'and exhorted them all that with purpose of heart they would cleave unto the Lord.'[2] As a preacher, he does not seem to have been equal to the apostle Paul; yet so far was he from caring about being eclipsed by Paul's superior abilities, that he went in search of him, and brought him to Antioch, to assist him in the work of the Lord. It may well be said of such a character, that he was a 'good man, and full of the Holy Spirit, and of faith.' Oh that we had more such ministers in the church at this day! Oh that we ourselves were like him! Might we not hope, if that were the case, that, according to God's usual manner of working, more people would be added to the Lord?

There are three things, we see, which are said of Barnabas in a way of commendation: he was 'a good man, full of the Holy Spirit, and of faith.' Thus far he is held up for our example: a fourth is added, concerning the effects which followed: 'and much people was added unto the Lord.' This seems to be held up for our encouragement. Permit me, my dear brother, to request your

2 Acts 11:23

candid attention, while I attempt to review these great qualities in Barnabas, and by every motive to enforce them upon you.

I. He was a good man.

It were easy to prove the necessity of a person being a good man, in order to his properly engaging in the work of the ministry: Christ would not commit his sheep but to one that loved him. But on this remark I shall not enlarge. I have no reason to doubt, my brother, but that God has given you an understanding to know him that is true, and a heart to love him in sincerity; I trust, therefore, such an attempt, on this occasion, is needless. Nor does it appear to me to be the meaning of the evangelist. It is not barely meant of Barnabas that he was a regenerate man, though that is implied; but it denotes that he was eminently good. We use the word so in common conversation. If we would describe one that more than ordinarily shines in piety, meekness, and kindness, we know not how to speak of him better than to say, with a degree of emphasis, 'He is a good man.' After this eminence in goodness, brother, may it be your concern, and mine, daily to aspire!

Perhaps, indeed, we may have sometimes heard this epithet used with a sneer. Persons who take pleasure in treating others with contempt will frequently, with a kind of proud pity, speak in this manner: 'Aye, such a one is a good man', leaving it implied that goodness is but an indifferent qualification, unless it be accompanied with greatness. But these things ought not to be. The apostle Paul did not value himself upon those things wherein he differed from other Christians; but upon that which he possessed in common with them—charity, or Christian love. 'Though I speak with the tongues of men and of angels, and have not charity, I am become as sounding brass, or a tinkling cymbal. And though I have the gift of prophecy, and understand all mysteries, and all knowledge; and though I have all faith, so that I could remove mountains, and have not charity; I am nothing.'[3]

My dear brother, value the character of a good man in all the parts of your employment; and, above all, in those things which the world counts great and estimable. More particularly:

1. Value it at home in your family. If you walk not closely with God there, you will be ill able to work for him elsewhere. You have lately become the head of a family. Whatever charge it shall please God, in the course of your life, to place under your care, I trust it will be your concern to recommend Christ and the gospel to them, walk circumspectly before them, constantly worship God with them, offer up secret prayer for them, and exercise a proper authority over them. There is a sort of religious gossiping which some ministers have indulged to their hurt; loitering about perpetually at the houses of their friends, and taking no delight in their own. Such conduct, in a minister and master of a family, must, of necessity, root out all family order, and, to a great degree, family worship; and, instead of endearing him to his friends, it only exposes him to their just censure. Perhaps they know not how to be so plain as to tell him of it at their own houses; but they will think the more, and speak of it, it is likely, to each other, when he is gone. I trust, my brother, that none of your domestic connections will have to say when you are gone, 'He was loose and careless in his conduct', or 'sour and churlish in his temper'; but rather, 'He was a good man.'

2. Value this character in your private retirements. Give yourself up to 'the word of God, and to prayer.'[4] The apostle charged Timothy, saying, 'Meditate on these things, give thyself wholly to them';[5] or, 'be thou in them.' But this will never be, without a

---

3 1 Corinthians 13:1–2.

4 Acts 6:4.

5 1 Timothy 4:15.

considerable share of the good man. Your heart can never be in those things which are foreign to its prevailing temper; and if your heart is not in your work, it will be a poor lifeless business indeed. We need not fear exhausting the Bible, or dread a scarcity of divine subjects. If our hearts are but kept in unison with the spirit in which the Bible was written, everything we meet with there will be interesting. The more we read, the more interesting it will appear; and the more we know, the more we shall perceive there is to be known. Beware also, brother, of neglecting secret prayer. The fire of devotion will go out if it be not kept alive by an habitual dealing with Christ. Conversing with men and things may brighten our gifts and parts; but it is conversing with God that must brighten our graces. Whatever ardour we may feel in our public work, if this is wanting, things cannot be right, nor can they in such a train come to a good issue.

3. Value it in your public exercises. It is hard going on in the work of the ministry, without a good degree of spirituality; and yet, considering the present state of human nature, we are in the greatest danger of the contrary. Allow me, brother, to mention two things in particular, each of which is directly opposite to that spirit which I am attempting to recommend. One is, an assumed earnestness, or forced zeal, in the pulpit, which many weak hearers may mistake for the enjoyment of God. But though we may put on violent emotions—may smite with the hand, and stamp with the foot—if we are destitute of a genuine feeling sense of what we deliver, it will be discerned by judicious hearers, as well as by the Searcher of hearts, and will not fail to create disgust. If, on the contrary, we feel and realize the sentiments we deliver, emotions and actions will be the natural expressions of the heart; and this will give weight to the doctrines, exhortations, or reproofs which we inculcate; what we say will come with a kind of divine authority to the consciences, if not to the hearts of the hearers. The other is, being under the influence of low and selfish motives in the

exercise of our work. This is a temptation against which we have especial reason to watch and pray. It is right, my brother, for you to be diligent in your public work; to be instant in season and out of season; to preach the gospel not only at Thorn, but in the surrounding villages, wherever a door is opened for you: but while you are thus engaged, let it not be from motives of policy, merely to increase your auditory, but from love to Christ and the souls of your fellow sinners. It is this only that will endure reflection in a dying hour. The apostle Paul was charged by some of the Corinthian teachers with being crafty, and with having caught the Corinthians with guile; but he could say, in reply to all such insinuations, in behalf of himself and his fellow-labourers, 'Our rejoicing is this, the testimony of our conscience, that in simplicity and godly sincerity, not with fleshly wisdom, but by the grace of God, we have had our conversation in the world.'[6]

4. Value it in the general tenor of your behaviour. Cultivate a meek, modest, peaceful, and friendly temper. Be generous and humane. Prove by your spirit and conduct that you are a lover of all mankind. To men in general, but especially to the poor and the afflicted, be pitiful, be courteous. It is this, my brother, that will recommend the gospel you proclaim. Without this, could you preach with the eloquence of an angel, you may expect that no good end will be answered.

5. Prize the character of the good man above worldly greatness. It is not sinful for a minister, any more than another man, to possess property; but to aspire after it is unworthy of his sacred character. Greatness, unaccompanied with goodness, is valued as nothing by the great God. Kings and emperors, where that is wanting, are but great beasts, horned beasts, pushing one at another. When Sennacherib vaunted against the church of God, that he would

6 2 Corinthians 1:12.

'enter the forest of her Carmel, and cut down her tall cedars',[7] the daughter of Zion is commanded to despise him. God speaks of him as we should speak of a buffalo, or even of an ass: 'I will put my hook in thy nose, and my bridle in thy lips, and I will turn thee back by the way by which thou camest.'[8] Outward greatness, when accompanied with goodness, may be a great blessing; yet, even then, it is the latter, and not the former, that denominates the true worth of a character.

Once more,

6. Value it above mental greatness, or greatness in gifts and parts.

It is not wrong to cultivate gifts; on the contrary, it is our duty so to do. But, desirable as these are, they are not to be compared with goodness. 'Covet earnestly the best gifts', says the apostle, 'and yet show I unto you a more excellent way'; viz, charity, or love.[9] If we improve in gifts and not in grace, to say the least, it will be useless, and perhaps dangerous, both to ourselves and others. To improve in gifts, that we may be the better able to discharge our work, is laudable; but if it be for the sake of popular applause, we may expect a blast. Hundreds of ministers have been ruined by indulging a thirst for the character of the great man, while they have neglected the far superior character of the good man.

Another part of the character of Barnabas was that,

II. He was full of the Holy Spirit.

The Holy Spirit sometimes denotes his extraordinary gifts, as in Acts 19, where the apostle Paul put the question to some believers in Christ whether they had received the Holy Spirit; but here it signifies his indwelling and ordinary operations, or what is

---

7 Isaiah 37:24.

8 Isaiah 37:29.

9 1 Corinthians 12:31.

elsewhere called 'an unction from the Holy One.'[10] This, though more common than the other, is far more excellent. Its fruits, though less brilliant, are abundantly the most valuable. To be able to surmount a difficulty by Christian patience is a greater thing in the sight of God than to remove a mountain. Every work of God bears some mark of Godhead, even a thistle, or a nettle; but there are some of his works which bear a peculiar likeness to his holy moral character: such were the minds of men and angels in their original state. This will serve to illustrate the subject in hand. The extraordinary gifts of the Holy Spirit are a communication of his power; but in his dwelling in the saints, and the ordinary operations of his grace, he communicates his own holy nature; and this it was of which Barnabas was full. To be full of the Holy Spirit is to be full of the dove, as I may say; or full of those fruits of the Spirit mentioned by the apostle to the Galatians; namely, 'love, joy, peace, long-suffering, gentleness, goodness.'[11]

To be sure, the term 'full' is not here to be understood in an unlimited sense; not in so ample a sense as when it is applied to Christ. He was filled with the Spirit without measure, but we in measure. The word is doubtless to be understood in a comparative sense, and denotes as much as that he was habitually under his holy influence. A person that is greatly under the influence of the love of this world is said to be drunken with its cares or pleasures. In allusion to something like this, the apostle exhorts that we 'be not drunken with wine, wherein is excess; but filled with the Spirit.'[12] The word 'filled', here, is very expressive; it denotes, I apprehend, being overcome, as it were, with the holy influences and fruits of the blessed Spirit. How necessary is all this, my brother, in your work! Oh how necessary is 'an unction from the Holy One!'

---

10 1 John 2:20.
11 Galatians 5:22.
12 Ephesians 5:18.

1. It is this that will enable you to enter into the spirit of the gospel, and preserve you from destructive errors concerning it. Those who have an unction from the Holy One are said to 'know all things; and the anointing which they have received abideth in them, and they need not that any man teach them, but as the same anointing teacheth them all things, and is truth, and is no lie.'[13] We shall naturally fall in with the dictates of that spirit of which we are full. It is for want of this, in a great measure, that the Scriptures appear strange, and foreign, and difficult to be understood. He that is full of the Holy Spirit has the contents of the Bible written, as I may say, upon his heart; and thus its sacred pages are easy to be understood, as 'wisdom is easy to him that understandeth.'[14]

It is no breach of charity to say, that if the professors of Christianity had more of the Holy Spirit of God in their hearts, there would be a greater harmony among them respecting the great truths which he has revealed. The rejection of such doctrines as the exceeding sinfulness of sin, the total depravity of mankind, the proper deity and atonement of Christ, justification by faith in his name, the freeness and sovereignty of grace, and the agency of the Holy Spirit, may easily be accounted for upon this principle. If we are destitute of the Holy Spirit, we are blind to the loveliness of the divine character, and destitute of any true love to God in our hearts; and if destitute of this, we shall not be able to see the reasonableness of that law which requires love to him with all the heart; and then, of course, we shall think lightly of the nature of those offences committed against him; we shall be naturally disposed to palliate and excuse our want of love to him, yea, and even our positive violations of his law; it will seem hard, very hard indeed, for such little things as these to be punished with everlasting destruction. And now, all this admitted, we

---

13 Cf. 1 John 2:27.
14 Proverbs 14:6.

shall naturally be blind to the necessity and glory of salvation by Jesus Christ. If sin is so trifling an affair, it will seem a strange and incredible thing that God should become incarnate to atone for it; and hence we shall be very easily persuaded to consider Christ as only a good man, who came into the world to set us a good example; or, at least, that he is not equal with the Father. The freeness and sovereignty of grace also, together with justification by imputed righteousness, will be a very strange sound in our ears. Like the Jews, we shall 'go about to establish our own righteousness, and shall not submit to the righteousness of God.'[15] It will seem equally strange and incredible to be told that we are by nature utterly unfit for the kingdom of God; that, therefore, we must be born again; that we are so bad that we cannot even come to Christ for life, except the Father draw us; yea, and that our best doings, after all, are unworthy of God's notice. It will be no wonder if, instead of receiving these unwelcome and humiliating doctrines, we should coincide with those writers and preachers who think more favourably of our condition, and the condition of the world at large; who either deny eternal punishment to exist, or represent men in general as being in little or no danger of it. And having avowed these sentiments, it will then become necessary to compliment their abettors (including ourselves in the number) as persons of a more rational and liberal way of thinking than other people.

My dear brother, of all things, be this your prayer, 'Take not thy Holy Spirit from me!'[16] If once we sink into such a way of performing our public work as not to depend on his enlightening and enlivening influences, we may go on, and probably shall go on, from one degree of evil to another. Knowing how to account for the operations of our own minds, without imputing them to a divine agency, we shall be inclined, in this manner, to account for

---

15 Romans 10:3.
16 Psalm 51:11.

the operations in the mind of others; and so, with numbers in the present age, may soon call in question even 'whether there be any Holy Spirit.'[17]

2. Being full of the Holy Spirit will give a holy tincture to your meditation and preaching. There is such a thing as the mind being habitually under the influence of divine things, and retaining so much of a savour of Christ as that divine truths shall be viewed and expressed, as I may say, in their own language. Spiritual things will be spiritually discerned, and if spiritually discerned, will be spiritually communicated. There is more in our manner of thinking and speaking upon divine truth than perhaps, at first sight, we are aware of. A great part of the phraseology of Scripture is by some accounted unfit to be addressed to a modern ear; and is, on this account, to a great degree laid aside, even by those who profess to be satisfied with the sentiments. Whatever may be said in defense of this practice, in a very few instances, such as those where words in a translation are become obsolete, or convey a different idea from what they did at the time of being translated, I am satisfied the practice in general is very pernicious. There are many sermons, that cannot fairly be charged with untruth, which yet have a tendency to lead off the mind from the simplicity of the gospel. If such Scripture terms, for instance, as 'holiness, godliness, grace, believers, saints, communion with God', etc., should be thrown aside as savouring too much of cant and enthusiasm, and such terms as morality, virtue, religion, good men, happiness of mind, etc., substituted in their room, it will have an amazing effect upon the hearers. If such preaching is the gospel, it is the gospel heathenized, and will tend to heathenize the minds of those who deal in it. I do not mean to object to the use of these latter terms, in their place; they are some of them Scriptural terms: what I object to is putting them in the place of others, when discoursing

_____

17 Acts 19:2.

upon evangelical subjects. To be sure, there is a way of handling divine subjects after this sort that is very clever and very ingenious; and a minister of such a stamp may commend himself, by his ingenuity, to many hearers: but, after all, God's truths are never so acceptable and savoury to a gracious heart as when clothed in their own native phraseology. The more you are filled, my brother, with an unction from the Holy One, the greater relish you will possess for that savoury manner of conveying truth which is so plentifully exemplified in the Holy Scriptures. Further,

3. It is this that will make the doctrines you preach, and the duties you inculcate, seem fitted in your lips. I allude to a saying of the wise man: 'The words of the wise are pleasant, if thou keep them within thee; they shall withal be fitted in thy lips.'[18] It is expected that there should be an agreement between the character of the speaker and the things which are spoken. 'Excellent speech becometh not a fool.'[19] Exhortations to holiness come with an ill grace from the lips of one who indulges himself in iniquity. The opposite of this is what I mean by the doctrines and duties of religion being fitted in your lips. It is this that will make your face shine, when you come forth in your public labours, like the face of Moses when he had been conversing with God in the holy mount.

4. It is this that will give a spiritual savour to your conversation in your visits to your friends. Though religious visits may be abused; yet you know, brother, the necessity there is for them, if you would ascertain the spiritual condition of those to whom you preach. There are many faults also that you may discover in individuals which it would be unhandsome, as well as unfriendly, to expose in a pointed manner in the pulpit, which nevertheless ought not to be passed by unnoticed. Here is work for your private visits; and, in proportion as you are filled with the Holy Spirit, you will possess

18 Cf. Proverbs 22:17–18.
19 Proverbs 17:7.

a spirit of love and faithfulness, which is absolutely necessary to successful reproof. It is in our private visits also that we can be free with our people, and they with us. Questions may be asked and answered, difficulties solved, and the concerns of the soul discussed. Paul taught the Ephesians, not only publicly, but 'from house to house.'[20] Now it is being full of the Holy Spirit that will give a spiritual savour to all this conversation. It will be as the holy anointing oil on Aaron's garments, which diffused a savour on all around him.

5. This will also teach you how you ought to behave yourself in every department you are called to occupy. It will serve instead of ten thousand rules; and all rules without it will be of no account. This it is that will teach you to be of a meek, mild, peaceful, humble spirit. It will make such a spirit be natural to you. 'As touching brotherly love', said the apostle to the Thessalonians, 'ye need not that I write unto you, for ye yourselves are taught of God to love one another.'[21]

6. In short, it is this that will denominate you the man of God. Such was Barnabas, and such, my brother, was your predecessor, whose memory is dear to many of us;[22] and such, according to all that I have heard, was his predecessor, whose memory is equally dear to many here present.[23] Each, in his day, was a burning and shining light; but they shine here no more. May you, my brother, and each of us, be followers of them, as they also were of Christ!

Another part of the character of Barnabas is,

III. He was full of faith.

It may be difficult to ascertain with precision the real meaning and extent of this term; but, I should think, in this connection

---

20 Acts 20:20.

21 1 Thessalonians 4:9.

22 David Evans was the minister of the Thorn congregation from 1781–1787.

23 William Buttfield served the Thorn congregation from 1775 to 1778.

it includes, at least, the three following ideas: having the mind occupied with divine sentiment; being rooted and grounded in the truth of the gospel; and daily living upon it. The first of these ideas distinguished him from those characters whose minds are void of principle; the next, from such as are always hovering upon the borders of skepticism; and the last, from those who, though they have no manner of doubts about the truth of the doctrines of the gospel, yet scarcely ever, if at all, feel their vital influence upon their hearts and lives. Let us review each of these a little more particularly.

1. His mind was well occupied, or stored, with divine sentiment. How necessary is this to a gospel minister! It is to be feared that many young men have rushed into the work of the Lord without any decided principles of their own; yea, and have not only begun in such a state of mind, but have continued so all through their lives. Alas! what can the churches expect from such characters? What can such a void produce? How can we feed others with knowledge and understanding if we ourselves are destitute of them? To say the least, such ministers will be but 'unprofitable servants.'[24] But this is not all; a minister that is not inured to think for himself is constantly exposed to every false sentiment, or system, that happens to be presented to him. We sometimes hear of a person changing his sentiments; and, doubtless, in many cases it is just and right he should change them: but there are cases in which that mode of speaking is very improper; for, in reality, some persons have no sentiments of their own to change; they have only changed the sentiments of some one great man for those of another.

2. He had a firm persuasion of the truth of that gospel which he preached to others. He was rooted and grounded in the gospel. The great controversy of that day was whether the gospel was

---

24 See Matthew 25:20.

true; whether Jesus was the Messiah; whether he, who so lately expired on the cross, was the Son of God; and whether his death was the way to obtain eternal life. There were great temptations for a person who should view things through a medium of sense to think otherwise. The popular opinion went against it. To the Jews it was a stumbling-block, and to the Greeks foolishness. Those who adhered to the gospel, thereby exposed themselves to cruel persecutions. But Barnabas was 'full of faith'; he was decidedly on the Lord's side; he 'believed on the Son of God', and had the 'witness 'of the truth of his gospel 'within himself.'[25]

Preaching the gospel is bearing a testimony for God; but we shall never be able to do this to any good purpose, if we be always hesitating and indulging a sceptical disposition. There is no need of a dogmatical, overbearing temper; but there is need of being rooted and grounded in the truths of God. 'Be not carried about', said the apostle to the Hebrews, 'with strange doctrines: it is a good thing that the heart be established with grace.'[26] But he elsewhere condemns the character of those who are 'ever learning, and never able to come to the knowledge of the truth.'[27]

3. That gospel which he preached to others he himself lived upon. 'The word preached', we are told, 'did not profit some, because it was not mixed with faith in them that heard it.'[28] This will equally hold good in the case of the preacher as of the hearer. If we mix not faith with the doctrine we deliver, it will not profit us. Whatever abilities we may possess, and of whatever use we may be made to others, unless we can say, in some sort, with the apostle John, 'That which we have seen with our eyes, and looked upon, and our hands have handled of the word of life—that declare we

---

25 1 John 5:10.
26 Hebrews 13:9.
27 2 Timothy 3:7.
28 Hebrews 4:2.

unto you',[29] our own souls may, notwithstanding, everlastingly perish! This is a very serious matter, and well deserves our attention as ministers. Professors in the age of Barnabas might be under greater temptations than we are to question whether Jesus was the true Messiah; but we are under greater temptations than they were of resting in a mere implicit assent to the Christian religion, without realizing and living upon its important truths.

The studying of divine truth as preachers rather than as Christians, or, in other words, studying it for the sake of finding out something to say to others, without so much as thinking of profiting our own souls, is a temptation to which we are more than ordinarily exposed. If we studied divine truths as Christians, our being constantly engaged in the service of God would be friendly to our growth in grace. We should be 'like trees planted by the rivers of waters, that bring forth fruit in their season', and all that we did would be likely to 'prosper.'[30] But if we study it only as preachers, it will be the reverse. Our being conversant with the Bible will be like surgeons and soldiers being conversant with the shedding of human blood, till they lose all sensibility concerning it. I believe it is a fact that, where a preacher is wicked, he is generally the most hardened against conviction of any character whatever. Happy will it be for us if, like Barnabas, we are 'full of faith' in that Saviour whom we recommend—in that gospel which it is our employment to proclaim.

IV. We now come to the last part of the subject, which is held up by way of encouragement: 'And much people was added unto the Lord.'
When our ministry is blessed to the conversion of sinners, to the bringing them off from their connection with sin and self to a vital union with Christ; when our congregations are filled,

---

29 1 John 1:1, 3.
30 Psalm 1:3.

not merely with professors of religion, but with sound believers; when such believers come forward and offer themselves willingly for communion, saying, 'We will go with you, for we have heard that God is with you';[31] then it may be said that 'much people is added unto the Lord.' The connection between such additions, and eminency in grace and holiness in a minister, deserves our serious attention.

I think it may be laid down as a rule, which both Scripture and experience will confirm, that eminent spirituality in a minister is usually attended with eminent usefulness. I do not mean to say our usefulness depends upon our spirituality, as an effect depends upon its cause; nor yet that it is always in proportion to it. God is a Sovereign; and frequently sees proper to convince us of it, in variously bestowing his blessing on the means of grace. But yet he is not wanting in giving encouragement to what he approves, wherever it is found. Our want of usefulness is often to be ascribed to our want of spirituality, much oftener than to our want of talents. God has frequently been known to succeed men of inferior abilities, when they have been eminent for holiness, while he has blasted others of much superior talents, when that quality has been wanting. Hundreds of ministers, who, on account of their gifts, have promised to be shining characters, have proved the reverse; and all owing to such things as pride, unwatchfulness, carnality, and levity.

Eminency in grace, my brother, will contribute to your success in three ways:

1. It will fire your soul with holy love to Christ and the souls of men; and such a spirit is usually attended with success. I believe you will find that, in almost all the great works which God has wrought, in any period of time, he has honoured men of this

---

31 Zechariah 8:23.

character, by making them his instruments. In the midst of a sore calamity upon the murmuring Israelites, when God was inclined to show mercy, it was by the means of his servant Aaron running with a censer of fire in his hand, and standing between the living and the dead! The great reformation that was brought about in the days of Hezekiah was by the instrumentality of a man 'who wrought that which was good and right and truth before the Lord his God';[32] and then it follows, 'and in every work that he began in the service of the house of God, and in the law, and in the commandments, to seek his God, he did it with all his heart, and prospered.'[33]

There was another great reformation in the Jewish church, about the time of their return from Babylon. One of the chief instruments in this work was Ezra, 'a ready scribe in the law of his God'[34]—a man who had 'prepared his heart to seek the law of the Lord, and to do it, and to teach in Israel statutes and judgments'[35]—a man who 'fasted and prayed at the river Ahava',[36] previously to his great undertaking—a man who was afterwards 'sorely astonished, and in heaviness, and would eat no meat, nor drink water, but fell upon his knees, and spread out his hands unto the Lord his God, on account of the transgressions of the people.'[37] Another great instrument in this work was Nehemiah, a man that devoted himself wholly to the service of God and his people, laboring night and day, and was not to be seduced by the intrigues of God's adversaries, nor yet intimidated by their threatenings; but persevered in his work till it was finished, closing his labors with

---

32 2 Chronicles 31:20.
33 2 Chronicles 31:21.
34 Ezra 7:6.
35 Ezra 7:10.
36 See Ezra 8:21.
37 See Ezra 9.

this solemn prayer and appeal, 'Think upon me, O my God, for good, according to all that I have done for this people.'[38]

Time would fail me to speak of all the great souls, both inspired and uninspired, whom the King of kings has delighted to honour: of Paul, and Peter, and their companions; of Wickliff, and Luther, and Calvin, and many others at the Reformation; of Elliot, and Edwards, and Brainerd, and Whitefield, and hundreds more whose names are held in deserved esteem in the church of God. These were men of God; men who had great grace, as well as gifts; whose hearts burned in love to Christ and the souls of men. They looked upon their hearers as their Lord had done upon Jerusalem, and wept over them. In this manner they delivered their messages; 'and much people were added unto the Lord.'

2. Eminency in grace will direct your ends to the glory of God, and the welfare of men's souls; and where this is the case, it is usually attended with a blessing.

These are ends which God himself pursues; and if we pursue the same, we are 'labourers together with God',[39] and may hope for his blessing to attend our labours; but if we pursue separate and selfish ends, we walk contrary to God, and may expect God to walk contrary to us. Whatever apparent success may attend the labours of a man whose ends are evil, all is to be suspected; either the success is not genuine, or, if it be, it is not in a way of blessing upon him, nor shall it turn out, at last, to his account. It must he an inexpressible satisfaction, brother, to be able to say as the primitive ministers and apostles did: 'James, a servant of God—Paul, a servant of Jesus Christ—We seek not yours, but you.'[40]

3. Eminency in grace will enable you to bear prosperity in your

---

38 Nehemiah 5:19.
39 1 Corinthians 3:9.
40 James 1:1; Romans 1:1; 2 Corinthians 12:14.

ministry without being lifted up with it; and so contribute towards it. It is written of Christ, in prophecy, 'He shall build the temple of the Lord, and shall bear the glory.'[41] He does bear it indeed; but to bear glory without being elated is no easy thing for us. I am often afraid lest this should be one considerable reason why most of us have no more real success in our work than we have; perhaps it is not safe for us to be much owned of God; perhaps we have not grace enough to bear prosperity.

My dear brother, permit me to conclude with a word or two of serious advice. First, watch over your own soul, as well as the souls of your people. Do not forget that ministers are peculiarly liable, while they keep the vineyard of others, to neglect their own. Further, know your own weakness, and depend upon Christ's all-sufficiency. Your work is great, your trials may be many; but let not your heart be discouraged. Remember what was said to the apostle Paul, 'My grace is sufficient for thee, my strength is made perfect in weakness'; and the reflection which he makes upon it, 'When I am weak, then am I strong.'[42] Finally, be often looking to the end of your course, and viewing yourself as giving an account of your stewardship. We must all appear before the judgment-seat of Christ, and give account of the deeds done in the body. Perhaps there is no thought more solemn than this, more suitable to be kept in view in all our undertakings, more awakening in a thoughtless hour, or more cheering to an upright heart.

I have only to request, my dear brother, that you will excuse the freedom of this plain address. I have not spoken so much to instruct you in things which you know not, as to remind and impress you with things which you already know. The Lord bless you, and grant that the solemnities of this day may ever be remembered with satisfaction, both by you and your people!

---

41 Zechariah 6:13.

42 2 Corinthians 12:9–10.

2. Pastors Required to Feed the Flock of Christ[43]

'Feed my sheep' (John 21:16).

The conversation which passed between our Lord and Peter, of which the text forms a part, was designed to administer reproof, and to communicate forgiveness. The cutting question was calculated to wound him to the quick; the kind direction amounted to a full forgiveness. He might expect he had lost his office—but no—he shall be restored. 'Feed my sheep.'

There are a few things suggested by these words which have of late made some impression on my mind; particularly, the love of Christ to his people—my own duty as a pastor—and the character necessary for you to sustain, if you would thrive under the Word.

Let me notice,

I. The love of Christ to his people, discovered in this charge to Peter.

You are to view him as a shepherd—the good Shepherd of the sheep—the chief Shepherd. The time also is worthy of notice; he had just laid down his life for the sheep; nay more, he had taken it again (Hebrews 13:20); and being now about to leave his flock in the world, as sheep among wolves, he commits them to his under-shepherd. There is a close connection between his having died for them and his desire to have them fed; which is afterward recognised by the apostle Paul, in his farewell address to the elders of the church at Ephesus 'Feed the church of God, which he hath purchased with his own blood.'[44]

Observe three things in particular:

1. The interest he claims in them: 'My sheep'—'my lambs.' They are his as given him by the Father, John 10:29. They are his as

---

43 *Complete Works*, I, 477–478.
44 Acts 20:28.

having purchased them with his blood, Acts 20:28. And they are his as being the travail of his soul, the reward of his death, which 'satisfied' him.

2. The qualification he requires in their shepherd—Love! He would not trust them with one who did not love him. One who did not love him, a hireling, would starve them, or poison them, and flee in a time of danger, John 10:12. Give him the fleece, the flock may care for themselves. But if we love Christ, we shall love his people for his sake. We shall feel a subordinate interest in them. It is by this a good shepherd is distinguished from a hireling, John 10:11. Love will inspire vigilance and boldness in feeding the flock, and defending them from danger. David was a genuine shepherd, when he risked his life to save a lamb.

3. The provision he has made for their being fed. Under-shepherds cannot furnish the pasture; the utmost we can do is to lead you into it. But Christ does more. He not only provides shepherds, but pasture—the gospel, of which he is the subject.

II. The duty of a minister to his people. It is to 'feed' them.
The word here rendered 'feed' signifies the whole duty of a shepherd, and not merely to supply them with food—to govern them, protect them, to care for them; or (as Peter himself expresses it) 'to take the oversight of them.'[45] To discharge this duty as it demands is a great matter.

1. It requires that we be divested of a selfish spirit. The description of an idol shepherd, by Zechariah (11:16–17), has of late been much on my mind. Two evils hang over him who is his own idol, or who wishes to be idolized by his people—a blast on his labours, and a mind void of judgment.

2. It requires that we be conversant with the gospel. How else can

---

45 See 1 Peter 5:2.

we lead others into it? If we be worldly-minded, we shall feed your evil principles and propensities, but not your graces; at best, only your mental faculties. Many are thus fed by ingenious, speculative preachers. But we must feed your best principles—your faith, hope, and love. Lord! who is sufficient for these things?

III. The character necessary for you to sustain in order to thrive under the Word.

You must be Christ's sheep, or you will not know his voice, the gospel will not be the food you will relish. If you are his sheep, you will enter in at the door. Christ is the door. You will know his voice, and follow him. You will enter his fold, uniting yourself to his people; and you will go in and out, and find pasture. You will enter into the spirit of the church, as described by Solomon: 'Tell me, O thou whom my soul loveth, where thou feedest; where thou makest thy flock to rest at noon', etc.[46]

Sustaining this character, you will not famish for want of food. The gospel is rich pasture. Having led you into it on earth, may I be able at last to give an account, both of you and myself, with joy, and not with grief!

---

46 Song of Solomon 1:7.

3. Spiritual Knowledge and Love Necessary for the Ministry[47]

'He was a burning and a shining light' (John 5:35).

In addressing you, my dear brother, on this solemn occasion, I shall not undertake so much to communicate anything new as to remind you of what you know, and have felt already. You are aware that there are two main objects to be attained in the work of the Christian ministry—*enlightening the minds* and *affecting the hearts* of the people. These are the usual means by which the work of God is accomplished. Allow me to remind you that, in order to the attainment of these objects, you yourself must be under their influence. If you would enlighten others, you must be 'a shining light' yourself. And if you would affect others, you yourself must feel; your own heart must 'burn' with holy ardour. You must be 'a *burning* and a *shining* light.'

It is not enough that you should be what is called a popular preacher. A man may have gifts, so as to shine in the eyes of the multitude, almost as bright as he does in his own eyes; and yet possess little or nothing of *spiritual* light—light, the tendency of which is to transform the heart. So also a man may burn with zeal, as Jehu did, and yet have little or no true love to God, or affection for the souls of men. *Spiritual light* and *holy love* are the qualities which Christ commends.

You will give your candid attention, my dear brother, while I endeavour to remind you of the necessity of each of these, in the different parts of your important work: in the great work of preaching the gospel—in presiding in the church—in visiting your people—and in your whole demeanour through life.

---

47 *Complete Works*, I, 478–482. This sermon can also be found in Keith S. Grant, *Andrew Fuller and the Evangelical Renewal of Pastoral Theology*, Studies in Baptist History and Thought, vol.36 (Milton Keynes: Paternoster, 2013), 126–130.

I. In the great work of preaching the Gospel.

O my brother, in this department we had need resemble the living creatures mentioned by Ezekiel, 'full of eyes' (1:18). We had almost need, in one view, to be made up of pure intellect—to be all light. I shall not attempt to decide how much knowledge is necessary, of men and things, of past and present times, of the church and the world; but shall confine myself to two or three particulars, as specimens.

1. How necessary is it to understand in some good degree the holy character of God! It is this to which you will find that men in general are blind. They conceive of God as if he were such a one as themselves ... And hence, they fancy they are not enemies to him. You will have to point out the true character of God, that the sinner may see his own deformity, and not have the enmity of his heart concealed from his eyes. A just view of the holy character of God will also be one of the best preservatives against error in other respects. Almost all the errors in the world proceed from ignorance of the true character of God. To what else can be attributed the errors of Socinianism, Arianism, and Antinomianism? From degraded views of God's character arise diminutive notions of the evil of sin—of its just demerit—of our lost condition—of our need of a great Saviour—and of the work of the Spirit. O my brother, may you shed abroad this light with unsullied lustre! And, in order to this, commune much with God in private; since there is no way of knowing the true character of another so well as by personal, private intercourse.

2. A knowledge of Christ, as the Mediator between God and man, is necessary.

'This is life eternal, to know thee, the only true God, and Jesus Christ whom thou hast sent.'[48] Here, also, men are greatly

---

48 John 17:3.

ignorant. He is in the world, and the world knows him not. It must be our concern, as ministers, to know him; and, comparatively speaking, 'to know nothing else' ... and this that we may diffuse the knowledge of him to others. The glory of Christ's character is such that if he were but viewed in a true light, and not through the false mediums of prejudice and the love of sin, but through the mirror of the gospel, he must be loved, John 4:29, 39–42. Here, my brother, we need to be intimately acquainted with Christ, that we may be able on all occasions to give him a just character— that we may be able to tell of his dignity, his love, the generous principles of his undertaking, and how nobly he executed the arduous enterprise.

3. A knowledge of human nature as created is necessary. We shall be unskillful workmen, unless we are acquainted with the materials on which we have to work. It is not more necessary for a surgeon or a physician to understand the anatomy of the human body, than it is for ministers to understand what may be called the anatomy of the soul. We had need enter into all the springs of action. In particular, we must be very careful to distinguish between primary and criminal passions. God habitually addresses the former, and so should we, but not the latter; the latter being only the abuse of the principles implanted in our nature. To be more explicit, God has created us with the love of possession, but the excess of this love becomes covetousness and idolatry. God has implanted within us a principle of emulation; but the abuse of this is pride and ambition. God has created us with the love of pleasure; but this indulged to excess becomes sensuality. Now the gospel never addresses itself to our corrupt passions; but the Word of God is full of appeals to those principles of our nature with which we are created. For example, in his Word, God addresses himself to our love of possession and points to 'an inheritance, incorruptible, undefiled,

and that fadeth not away'[49]—to the principle of emulation and presents to our view 'a crown'[50]—to our love of pleasure and informs us that 'in his presence there is fulness of joy, and at his right hand are pleasures for evermore.'[51] And, in short, in the same way, he addresses the principles of zeal, love, hatred, shame, fear, revenge, etc. And so must we.

4. A knowledge of human nature as depraved is necessary. Without this knowledge, we shall be unable to trace and detect the workings of a wicked heart. Sin is a deceitful thing, and we are apt to be imposed upon by its specious names. Parsimoniousness is called frugality; prodigality, generosity; bitterness of spirit in reproving, fidelity; and resentment, a becoming spirit. We need therefore to know the root of the disease, and the various ways in which it operates. In order to effect a cure, the knowledge of the disease is indispensable; and in order to attain to this knowledge, we must study the various symptoms by which the disorder may be distinguished.

5. A knowledge of human nature as sanctified by the Spirit is necessary.

Without this, we shall be unable to trace the work of God in the soul; and unable to fan the gentle flame of divine love in the genuine Christian, and to detect and expose the various counterfeits.

You will need also, my brother, a heart *warmed* with divine things, or you will never be 'a burning and a shining light.' When we are thinking or preaching, we need to *burn*, as well as shine. When we study, we may rack our brains, and form plans; but unless 'our hearts burn within us',[52] all will be a mere skeleton—our

---

49 1 Peter 1:4.
50 Cf. 2 Timothy 4:8.
51 Psalm 16:11.
52 Luke 24:32.

thoughts mere bones; whatever be their number, they will be all dry—very dry; and if we do not feel what we say, our preaching will be poor dead work. Affected zeal will not do. A gilded fire may shine, but it will not warm. We may smite with the hand, and stamp with the foot, and throw ourselves into violent agitations; but if we feel not, it is not likely the people will—unless, indeed, it be a feeling of disgust. But suppose there be no affectation, nor any deficiency of good and sound doctrine; yet if in our work we feel no inward satisfaction, we shall resemble a mill-stone—preparing food for others, the value of which we are unable to appreciate ourselves. Indeed, without feeling, we shall be incapable of preaching any truth or of inculcating any duty aright. How can we display the evil of sin, the love of Christ, or any other important truth, unless we feel it? How can we preach against sin, without feeling a holy indignation against it? It is this that will cause us, while we denounce sin, to weep over the sinner. Otherwise, we may deal in flings and personalities; but these will only irritate; they will never reclaim. O! If ever we do any good in our work, it must be the effect of love to God and love to men—love to the souls of men, while we detest, and expose, and denounce their sins. How could Paul have pursued his work with the ardour and intenseness which he manifested, if his heart had not burned with holy love?

II. Spiritual light and holy love are equally necessary in presiding in the Church of God.

Wisdom and love are necessary, calmly to lay down rules of discipline—to solve difficult questions—to prepare and digest, in concurrence with the deacons, such matters as require to be laid before the church—to nip little differences in the bud—to mediate between contending parties, etc. My brother, think of the example of the Lord Jesus, who, in his intercourse with his disciples, saluted them with this benediction, 'Peace be with you!'[53] The

---

53 John 20:21.

great art of presiding in a church, so as to promote its welfare, is
to be neutral between the members, always on the side of God and
righteousness, and to let them see that, whatever your opinion may
be, you really love them.

III. These qualities are necessary in the more private duty of visiting the people.

A considerable part of the pastoral office consists in visiting the
people, especially the afflicted. Paul could appeal to the elders
of the church at Ephesus, that he had taught them publicly and
'from house to house.'[54] It is of great consequence that, in your
pastoral visits, you should preserve the character of 'a burning and
a shining light.' Pastoral visits should not degenerate into religious
gossiping—a practice in which some have indulged to the disgrace
of religion. Unused to habits of reflection, they feel no relish for
solitude; and therefore, to employ the time which hangs so heavy
on their hands, they saunter about to see their friends, and to ask
them how they are. Nor is this the worst. Satan promptly furnishes
a subject where there is such a dearth; and hence gossiping has
generally produced tales of slander, and practices which have
proved a scandal to the Christian name! I trust, my brother, you
know the preciousness of time too well to squander it away in
idle visits. And yet visiting is an essential part of your work, that
you may become acquainted with the circumstances, the spiritual
necessities of your people. They will be able to impart their feelings
freely and unreservedly; and you will be able to administer the
appropriate counsel to much better purpose than you possibly
can from the pulpit, and with greater particularity than would be
becoming in a public address. Only let us burn while we shine.
Let a savour of Christ accompany all our instructions. A minister
who maintains an upright, affectionate conduct, may say almost
anything, in a way of just reproof, without giving offence.

---

54 Acts 20:20.

IV. Spiritual light and holy love are necessary in your whole demeanour through life.

May you, my brother, shine in holy wisdom, and burn with ardent love. Your will need them, wherever you go—in whatever you engage—that you may walk as one of the children of light.

Allow me to point out a few things which I have found of use, to conduce to these ends:

1. Read the lives of good men—the lives of such men as God has distinguished for gifts, and graces, and usefulness. Example has a great influence. The Scriptures abound with such examples. And, blessed be God, we have some now.

2. Study the Word of God, above all other books, and pray over it. It is this will set our hearts on fire. There are no such motives exhibited anywhere as there—no such exhibitions of wisdom and love.

3. Read men, as well as books, and your own heart, in order that you may read others. Copyists, you know, are generally bunglers. There is nothing that equals what is taken immediately from the life. We need always be making our observations, wherever we are, or wherever we go. If we get a system of human nature, or experience, or anything else, from books, rather than from our own knowledge, it will be liable to two disadvantages. First, it is not likely to be so near the truth; for systems which go through several hands are like successive copies of a painting, every copy of the preceding one is more unlike the original—or like the telling of a tale, the circumstances of which you do not know of your own personal knowledge: every time it is repeated there is some variation, and thus it becomes further removed from the truth. Thus, Agrippa showed his wisdom, when, instead of depending on the testimony of others, he determined to hear Paul himself. Secondly, if it be correct, still it will not be so serviceable to you

as if it were a system of your own working. Saul's armour might be better than David's sling; but not to him, seeing he had not proved it.

4. Live the life of a Christian, as well as of a minister. Read as one, preach as one, converse as one—to be profited, as well as to profit others. One of the greatest temptations of a ministerial life is to handle divine truth as ministers, rather than as Christians—for others, rather than for ourselves. But the Word will not profit them that preach it, any more than it will them that hear it, unless it be 'mixed with faith.'[55] If we study the Scriptures as Christians, the more familiar we are with them, the more we shall feel their importance; but if our object be only to find out something to say to others, our familiarity with them will prove a snare. It will resemble that of soldiers, and doctors, and undertakers with death; the more familiar we are with them, the less we shall feel their importance. See Proverbs 22:17–18; Psalm 1:2–3.

5. Commune with God in private. Walking with God in the closet is a grand means, with his blessing, of illuminating our minds and warming our hearts. When Moses came down from the mount, his face shone bright, and his heart burned with zeal for the honour of God and the good of his people. Alas! alas! for want of this ... See Jeremiah 10:21.

6. Hold forth the word of life, not only by precept, but by a holy practice. 'Let your light so shine before men, that they, seeing your good works, may glorify your Father who is in heaven.'[56] Without this, in vain will be all our pretensions to being 'burning and shining lights.'

My dear brother, allow me to conclude with an earnest prayer, that you may long continue a 'burning and a shining light' to this

---

55 Hebrews 4:2.
56 Matthew 5:16.

church; and that, after having 'turned many to righteousness', you may shine as a distinguished star in the firmament for ever and ever!

4. On an Intimate and Practical Acquaintance with the Word of God[57]

'Ezra had prepared his heart to seek the law of the Lord, and to do it, and to teach in Israel statutes and judgments' (Ezra 7:10).

My dear brother, the long and intimate friendship which has subsisted between us will, I hope, render any apology unnecessary for my occupying this situation upon this solemn occasion. I should certainly have felt a pleasure in hearing some senior minister; but with your desire, on the ground of intimate friendship, I feel disposed to comply. I feel a peculiar pleasure in addressing you, for I can speak to you as a friend—a brother—an equal—an acquaintance, with whom I have often taken sweet counsel and walked to the house of God. You will not, I am sure, misinterpret my freedom, or suppose that I wish to assume any superiority over you or to dictate to you. You expect me to insist upon the importance of the work in which you are engaged. And for this purpose I have directed my attention to the passage I have read and would recommend to you the example of Ezra.

Example has a strong tendency to excite us to emulation. And in Ezra the scribe you have the character of an eminent servant of the Most High God held up to your admiration and imitation. Ministers in the New Testament are called 'scribes, instructed unto the kingdom of heaven',[58] and in Ezra you have the character of 'a ready scribe.'[59] There are four things in his character upon which I shall discourse, and which I would recommend to you.

I. Seek the law, or will, of God.

I need not inform you, my brother, that the Law, in the Old Testament especially, is commonly to be understood as

---

57 *Complete Works*, I, 483–486.

58 Matthew 13:52.

59 Ezra 7:6.

synonymous with the Scriptures, the Word, or the revealed will of God. The Scriptures were then as commonly called 'the Law of the Lord'[60] as they are now called 'the *word* of God.'[61] So the term is to be understood here. To 'seek the law of the Lord' is the same as to ascertain his mind and will in his sacred word.

You are to 'feed the people with knowledge and understanding',[62] but you cannot do this without understanding yourself. Your lips are to 'keep knowledge', and the people are to 'seek the law at your mouth.'[63] But, in order to communicate it to them, you must seek it at the mouth of God.

1. Seek it, my brother. It will never be found without. It is a mine, in which you will have to dig. And it is a precious mine, which will well repay all your labour.

2. Seek it at the fountain-head. You feel, I doubt not, a great esteem for many of your brethren now living, and admire the writings of some who are now no more, and you will read their productions with attention and pleasure. But whatever excellence your brethren possess, it is all borrowed and it is mingled with error. Learn your religion from the Bible. Let that be your decisive rule. Adopt not a body of sentiments, or even a single sentiment, solely on the authority of any man—however great, however respected. Dare to think for yourself. Human compositions are fallible. But the Scriptures were written by men who wrote as they were inspired by the Holy Spirit. Human writings on religion resemble preaching. They are useful only so far as they illustrate the Scriptures, and induce us to search for them for ourselves.

3. Seek the will of God in every part of the Bible. It is very true that some parts of the Bible are more interesting than others. But

---

60 See, e.g., Psalm 19:7.
61 See, e.g., Hebrews 4:12.
62 Jeremiah 3:15.
63 Malachi 2:7.

'*all* Scripture is profitable'[64] and necessary. Do not take this part
and leave that. Some people foolishly talk of Arminian texts and
Calvinistic texts, as if Scripture were repugnant to itself! That
system, whatever it be called, cannot be the right one, that rejects
any one part of Scripture whatever.

4. Seek it perseveringly. Do not reckon yourself so to have found
it as to be self-sufficient. Be open to conviction from every quarter.
Seek it by reading, by meditation, by prayer, by conversation, by all
the means that offer. Do not reject information from an inferior,
or even an enemy. In the study of the Scriptures you will always be
a learner.

II. Prepare your heart to seek the law of the Lord.

There is a preparation of heart in which we are wholly *passive*,
which is, in the strictest sense, the work of God, and, without this,
woe be to any of us that should dare to set up for teachers of his
law and gospel! But there is also a preparation of heart in which
we are *active*; and this is the preparedness intended in the text.
In this, even, God is the cause: he actuates, but then we act. Of
this preparation we have to speak, and it consists in prayer, and
self-examination, and meditation. Your work is a course, and for
this you must prepare by 'girding up the loins of your mind'[65]—a
fight, and you must 'put on the whole armour of God.'[66] The work
of God should not be entered upon rashly. God frequently brings
his servants through a train of instructions and trials that they may
be fitted for it. Moses was forty years at court and forty years a
shepherd. These were his days of preparation. Christ prepared his
disciples by his instructions during his life, and previous to their
great work they prepared themselves, Acts 1.

Such preparation of heart is not only necessary for your entrance

---

64 2 Timothy 3:16.
65 1 Peter 1:13.
66 Ephesians 6:11.

into the pastoral office, but also for your continuance in it. You will find that every exercise requires it. You do not need being guarded against that erroneous notion of so trusting to the Spirit as to neglect personal preparation for your public labours. But this preparedness is not only requisite for speaking the truth in public, but as well for seeking it in private. Let all your private meditations be mingled with prayer. You will study your Bible to wonderful advantage, if you go to it spiritually-minded. It is this which causes us to see the beauty and to feel the force of many parts of Scripture, to which, in a carnal state of mind, we are blind and stupid. If we go to the study of the Bible wise in our own conceits and self-sufficient, we shall get no good. When we would be taught from God's Word, we must learn as little children.

Again, if we go to the Bible merely, or chiefly, to find something to say to the people, without respect to our own souls, we shall make but poor progress. My brother, study divine truth as a Christian and not merely as a minister. Consider your own soul as deeply interested, and dread the thought of cultivating others, while you suffer your own heart to remain uncultivated. If you study divine truth as a Christian, your being constantly engaged in the study will promote your growth in grace. You will be like 'a tree planted by rivers of water.'[67] You will not only bring forth fruit for the people, but your leaf shall not wither, and whatever you do shall prosper. But if merely as a minister, the reverse. I believe it is a fact, that where a minister is wicked, he is the most hardened against conviction of any character.

III. Keep the law.
'Do it.' The apostle Paul, in writing to Timothy, is very particular as to personal religion, in a bishop, or pastor. 'Take heed to thyself,

---

67 Psalm 1:3.

and to the doctrine.'[68] 'Keep thyself pure.'[69] 'Be thou an example of the believers, in word, in conversation, in charity, in spirit, in faith, in purity.'[70] Observe, too, the connection in which this exhortation stands. 'Let no man despise thy youth',[71] plainly intimating that a holy example will render even youth respectable. Your Lord and Master both did and taught the will of God.

1. Dread nothing more than recommending that to your people to which you do not attend yourself. You may preach with the fervour of an angel. But if your practice, your habitual deportment, be inconsistent, all you do will be in vain.

2. More is expected from you than from others. A wicked preacher is of all characters the most contemptible. Even the profane despise him.

3. You will attend to practical preaching. But how can you either exhort or reprove, if your people should ever have it in their power to say, 'Physician, heal thyself!';[72] 'Thou that teachest another, teachest thou not thyself!'[73]

4. Attend not only to such duties as fall under the eye of man, but walk with God in your family and in your closet. It will require all your wisdom to bring up your children 'in the nurture and admonition of the Lord.'[74] And if you rule not well in your own house, you cannot expect to maintain a proper influence in the church of God. Beware also of omitting secret devotions. Conversing with men and things may brighten your gifts; but communion with God is necessary to improve your graces.

---

68 1 Timothy 4:16.
69 1 Timothy 5:22.
70 1 Timothy 4:12.
71 1 Timothy 4:12.
72 Luke 4:23.
73 Romans 2:21.
74 Ephesians 6:4.

IV. Teach in Israel the statutes and judgments of God.

It is not for me to dictate to you what doctrines you are to teach or what precepts you should enforce. But I hope you will evince your sincerity by preaching in the main such things as in your confession of faith you have just avowed; not, however, to the neglect of other points, which could scarcely be expected to be introduced in such a document. The more you are acquainted with the Word of God, the more you will find it abounds with truths, reviving truths too, which seldom or never have a place in confessions of faith. But, passing this, allow me to give you a few general hints on the subject of teaching.

1. Let Christ and his apostles be your examples. Teach as they taught. It would be worth while to read over the Gospels and the Acts of the Apostles, if it were only to discover their manner of teaching. Dare to avow every truth which they avowed. And address your audience in such language as they addressed to theirs, and that without softening it down, or explaining it away.

2. Give every part of the truth its due proportion. Preach every truth in the proportion in which it is introduced by God in his Word. You will find some people attached to one class of truths and others to another class. But be you attached to all. If you are habitually dwelling upon one truth, it must be to the neglect of others. And it is at your peril to keep back any part of the counsel of God! If you preach not the great doctrines of the gospel, such as the entire depravity of our nature, the atonement of Christ, the work of the Spirit, etc., the people of God will be famished. If you preach these doctrines to the neglect of close practical addresses, they will be in danger of a religious surfeit. If you preach doctrinally, some may call you an Antinomian. If you preach practically, others may call you a legalist. But go on, my brother. This is a kind of dirt that won't stick. Preach the law evangelically

and the gospel practically, and God will bless you and make you a blessing.

3. Dare to teach unwelcome truths. The Christian ministry must be exercised with affection and fidelity. Study not to offend any man. Yet, keep not back important truth, even if it do offend. You must not enter the pulpit to indulge your own temper. But neither are you at liberty to indulge in the humour of others. Be more concerned to commend yourself to the consciences of your people than to their good opinion.

4. Give Scriptural proof of what you teach. Do not imagine that mere assertion will do. Evidence ought to form the body of your discourses. Such expressions as 'I say', uttered in the most magisterial tones, will, after all, prove nothing except the unwarrantable confidence of the preacher.

5. Consider yourself as standing engaged to teach all that hear you: rich and poor, young and old, godly and ungodly—'warning the wicked, lest his blood be required at your hands.'[75] Seek the salvation of every man's soul. This was the apostolic method: 'warning every man, and teaching every man in wisdom.'[76] Whether every individual of your congregation will accept your message is another question. Your concern should be, not to intermeddle with what is not revealed, but to 'preach the gospel to every creature',[77] and to pray for all, as Paul did for Agrippa and his court, without distinction: 'I would that [...] all that hear me this day were [...] altogether such as I am.'[78]

6. Teach privately as well as publicly. Make your visits among your people subservient to instruction and edification. Take the example of Paul, Acts 20:20. Let a savour of Christ accompany you

---

75 See Ezekiel 3:18.
76 Colossians 1:28.
77 Mark 16:15.
78 Acts 26:29.

in your intercourse with your flock. This will greatly contribute to your public usefulness.

My brother, seek the law of God—seek it with a prepared heart—reduce it to practice—and teach it diligently. And you will be, not only, like Ezra, a 'ready' scribe, but 'a scribe well-instructed in the kingdom of God.'[79]

---

79 Ezra 7:6; Matthew 13:52.

5. Ministers Appointed to Root out
Evil, and to Cultivate Good[80]

'I have this day set thee over the nations, and over the kingdoms, to root out, and to pull down, and to destroy, and to throw down, and to build, and to plant' (Jeremiah 1:10).

This language, my brother, is not in every sense applicable to the present occasion. The prophet's was an extraordinary, yours is an ordinary office. His was to be exercised over nations and kingdoms, yours over a church and congregation. Yet, even in his case, there was no civil power—he was no pope—nor was he invested with the authority of a modern bishop. All the power he had pertained to his office as a prophet; he had no secular authority; he pulled down and built up prophetically. And though you have no such power as this, by extraordinary inspiration, yet, in a way of declaring the truths of God's word, 'whose soever sins you remit, they are remitted, and whose soever sins you retain, they are retained.'[81]

Your labour is less than the prophet's was, but the nature of your work is much the same; and the same spirit of faithfulness is required over a few things as over many things.

Your work is divided into two parts. One is, to discourage evil: 'to root out, to pull down, to destroy, and to throw down.' The other is, to encourage good: 'to build, and to plant.'

The imagery, you perceive, is of two kinds—that of a house, and that of a garden.

The church is God's house, God's building; and you are appointed to be a labourer 'together with God',[82] to pull down,

80 *Complete Works*, I, 486–489.
81 John 20:23.
82 1 Corinthians 3:9.

and destroy, and throw down the rubbish, and then to build upon a new and good foundation.

The church is also God's garden; and you are appointed to work in it, and keep it in order, to root out the weeds, and to plant and cultivate the goodly fruit.

Give me your attention, my dear brother, while I inquire what are the evils you are to oppose, and the good you are to encourage, and the methods to be adopted in pursuing these objects. Let us,

I. Inquire what are the evils against which you must contend, and the methods you are to adopt in their opposition.

1. By your public ministry root out errors in doctrine. Overturn them—not by empty declamation, but by solid Scriptural evidence—not by the wild fury of a bigot, but with the pure love of the Christian pastor, whose care it should be to preserve his charge from things that tend to the ruin of their souls. Particularly, if you love God, you will be concerned to root up everything that opposes the glory of his character and moral government. Vindicate the ways of God to men against all their hard thoughts and speeches. Vindicate his law, both in its precepts and penalty. You have observed, I doubt not, that this is the foundation for the grace of the gospel. If you love Christ, you will root up those principles which degrade his dignity and set aside his atonement. If you love your people, you will root up those principles which endanger the salvation of their souls, such as self-righteousness and presumptuous hope. There is plenty of work to remove the covering and to pull down the vain expectations of sinners. [...] You have seen, and will see, many whose habitual deportment proves them enemies to the cross, who yet entertain hopes of heaven: try and find out the delusive ground of their hope, and expose it; only be careful to avoid personalities, which will irritate rather than convince.

2. By leading the church, in the exercise of faithful discipline, root out evil-doers. Churches which in former years have been respectable and prosperous are fast falling into decay for want of discipline. Some have pleaded the parable of the wheat and tares as an excuse for negligence in discipline; but this is a perversion. The field is the world, not the church. The application of the principle to the church would render all the rules of the gospel superfluous.

3. By rendering your occasional visits subservient to the purposes of conviction and correction. You may in this way root up many evils which you cannot by either of the other means. There are cases which you cannot touch in the pulpit, on account of their singularity and minuteness, without being personal, which, as I just said, will irritate rather than reclaim. There are also cases which do not fall under church censure, which yet should come within the cognizance of a faithful pastor. This, I confess, is a difficult part of your work; and some, for fear of giving offence, have declined it: but suppose offence were given, if you are in the path of duty, what have you to fear? Some will say, 'If such and such persons are offended, the cause will sink.' Then let it sink. You may safely leave that, however, to Christ; if it should therefore sink, he will not blame you. But what cause must that be that is upheld by such unworthy means? After all, however, there is a way of managing these things by which offence is seldom or ever given. The great secret is to mingle love with your fidelity. This was Paul's method with the Corinthians. Consider the peculiar temptations and constitutional or educational tendencies of the party, and mingle counsel and encouragement with censure. We proceed to inquire.

II. What is that good which you are to encourage, or what is the work denoted by building and planting? This is a much more agreeable part of the subject than the other, though not more necessary.

In general, encourage and impart just sentiments. The truth has ever been God's honoured instrument in doing good. Encourage and cultivate holy tempers and dispositions. Labour to build up your people in these things. That is not always the best ministry that draws the most followers, but that which does the most good. When I see a company of modest, humble, upright, lovely, diligent, holy people, I see the best evidence of a good minister. But let me be a little more particular.

First, as a *builder.*

1. Be sure that you lay a right foundation. Christ is the foundation of God's laying, the foundation of the apostles and prophets; and you must lay him, as the foundation of faith and holiness. All true holiness is built upon faith in Christ. Many preachers who profess to entertain a great regard for a holy life, and deal much in moral declamations, omit this part of their work.

2. See that your materials be fitly framed together, Ephesians 2:21. Three things belong to this: (1) That the materials be hewed and squared. What would a company of proud, self-willed, prejudiced professors do together with the godly? These sins must be cut off. They ought to be like the stones of the temple before you lay them in the house of God. (2) That they be formed by the same rule. The stones must not only be cut even, but so as to fit the foundation and each other, or they cannot be fitly framed. Whatever variety there may be in some respects, there must be uniformity in others. No society can exist without similarity of views. Our hearts must be renewed after the image of Christ; and if they fit and fall in with his gospel and government, they will fit one another. But all attempts to build men into religious society without this will be vain. 'For what fellowship hath righteousness with unrighteousness? And what communion hath light with darkness?' etc. See 2 Corinthians 6:14–18. 'How can two walk

together except that they be agreed?'[83] (3) That, in being placed in the building, everyone be put in that situation for which he is formed. Some have splendid gifts, and are like stones in the front of the building, for ornament and strength. Others have more private excellences; but, though less conspicuous, they may not be less useful. Some are like Barnabas, affectionate; and excel in seeking out obscure humble inquirers, Acts 9:27. Others are wise in counsel and grave in deportment. Every gift should be so disposed of as that it shall be of the greatest use to the whole, otherwise the building will not be fitly framed together. Where offices are filled with men because they are men of property, it is often otherwise.

3. So frame the whole as that it may be a fit habitation for God. It must be God's house, not yours. Beware that you go not about it as Nebuchadnezzar went about Babylon. 'This is the house which I have built'—this is my house! I trust you have no greater desire than that God would take up his abode with you. Well-build you but upon his foundation, and by his rule, and he will dwell with you. All buildings are with a view to habitation.

Secondly, as a *planter*, prepare the soil by searching and convincing doctrine. Sow 'wholly a right seed.'[84] When you see the plants growing up, give attention to them. Cultivate them by every means, and pray that they may be watered by the Holy Spirit.

Allow me a word or two, my brother, particularly applicable to yourself individually.

1. While you root out and pull down, and build and plant, in God's house and vineyard, do not overlook your own. Personal religion is of the utmost importance to a minister.

2. Take into consideration that you are 'a labourer together with

---

83 Amos 3:3.
84 Jeremiah 2:21.

God.'[85] He that employs you will reward you. Look, my brother, beyond the grave for your reward. We have but little here; but if we had much, it would be an awful thing to receive that for our reward!

---

85 1 Corinthians 3:9.

6. Ministers should be Concerned not to be Despised[86]

'Let no man despise thee' (Titus 2:15).

My brother, I feel a pleasure in the work of this day, partly from the love I bear to you, and partly from the love I feel towards the church. I trust you will receive a word of advice on this solemn occasion with candour and attention.

You will observe the passage is not an address to the people, not to despise their minister; but to the minister, not to be despised by the people. If you ask how you are to prevent this, I answer, contempt is not a voluntary feeling. It is not in the power of men to despise some characters. They may dislike them; they may affect to ridicule them; but they cannot in their hearts despise them. If a minister conducts himself in character, no man will be able to despise him. This, then, is the sentiment which I wish to impress upon you.

Your work as a pastor may be distinguished into three departments—the pulpit, the church, and the world—in each of which I hope you will so conduct yourself as that no man shall be able to despise you. Let me offer to your consideration a few particulars under each.

I. What concerns you *in the pulpit*, or in the work of preaching the gospel.

1. Avoid all affectation in your manner. Do not affect the man of learning by useless criticisms: many do this, only to display their knowledge. Nor yet the orator, by high-sounding words, or airs, or gestures. Useful learning and impressive delivery should by no means be slighted; but they must not be affected, or men will be sure to despise you.

---

86 *Complete Works*, I, 489–491.

2. Avoid self-seeking in your ends. Preach not yourself, but Christ Jesus. Seek not the approbation of men for yourself, but for your doctrine. Study to commend the gospel to the consciences of your hearers, rather than to your own orthodoxy, or ingenuity, or zeal, to their admiration. If, instead of your endeavouring to secure their reception of the gospel message, you are concerned to recommend yourself to their applause, you will be sure to be despised.

3. Avoid vulgarity and love wit. Though the pulpit is not the place for affected pomposity, neither is it the place for mean and low language. Few men are more contemptible than those who study to introduce vulgar nonsense and jocose anecdotes, to make people laugh. Sound speech, sound sense, and the greatest seriousness, adorn the pulpit. Without these, you will be despised.

4. Do not advance sentiments without being able to support them by Scripture evidence. Many content themselves with assertions without proof, and make vehemence supply the place of evidence. But this will cause you to be despised by men of understanding.

5. Beware that you do not preach an unfelt Gospel. If you do, it will be seen, and you will be despised. It will be seen that, though you affect to be in earnest, you do not feel; and that you scarcely believe your own doctrine. We may get into a habit of talking for the truth, and pleading for holiness, and yet be dead ourselves; and if so, we shall be sure to be despised.

6. Let not the fear of man deter you from declaring the whole counsel of God. Insist on every divine truth and duty. Where interest or friendship stand in the way, it may be trying; but if you yield, the very parties to whom you yield will despise you. Speak but the truth in love, and speak the whole truth, and you

will commend yourself to every man's conscience, when you can do no more.

7. Never degrade the pulpit by indulging in personalities. These are for private admonition. 'Rebuke with all authority';[87] but let your personal rebukes be private. To introduce them in the pulpit is unmanly, and would render you despicable. Let us apply the language.

II. To your behaviour *in the Church*, and *among your fellow Christians.*

1. Do not lord it over God's heritage. You will have to preside in the church, and direct its measures; but never assume the lordly priest. Expect your judgment, in some cases, to be overruled, and learn to yield with cheerfulness when the measures you wish to introduce appear to be opposed to the opinion and desires of the majority of your brethren. It is not with a minister of the gospel as with a minister of state—that he must have a majority, or he cannot stand his ground. If we 'look on the things of others',[88] we may, in non-essentials, after speaking our minds, yield and be happy. But if we are determined to carry every point which appears to us desirable, in spite of the opinion of our brethren, though we may not always succeed, we shall invariably be despised for the attempt.

2. Yet have a judgment of your own. This will become you on every subject; and where it is of importance you ought to be firm and resolute. A minister must not be borne down by the capriciousness of a few. He who is easily turned aside from a good object, and will bear insult without a proper manifestation of his displeasure, will be despised as much as a lordly high priest. If a minister be not firm, discipline will, in many cases, be neglected. People have their friends, and relatives, and favourites; and very

---

87 Titus 2:15.
88 Philippians 2:4.

few, though the operation be bloodless, have sufficient regard for rectitude to act upon the principle of the sons of Levi. See Exodus 32:17–29. But you must, or you will be despised.

3. Do not affect the gentleman in your visits. Do not assume airs of consequence, and take liberties in families, as if, because you are a minister, you are therefore superior as a man. I do not say, do not be a gentleman; but do not affect the great man. Real gentility, and urbanity, and politeness are no mean or despicable attainments. There was much Christian politeness in the apostle Paul. But the affectation of the fine gentleman is great folly; and no men are more despised than those who strut about with lordly dignity, and give themselves consequential airs. You had much better feel yourself a Christian, and consider that you are associating with your fellow Christians, or with those who expect you to exhibit a pattern for their imitation.

4. Yet preserve a dignity of manner and demeanour. There is no occasion for you, in order to avoid the affectation of gentility, to sink into low buffoonery, vulgarity, or drollery. My brother, the fear of God, and a deep sense of religion, will effectually preserve you from these extremes, and render you respectable, instead of contemptible.

5. Beware of being a loiterer. Do not acquire a habit of wandering about and doing nothing. Visit, and visit 'from house to house.'[89] But look well to your visits: '*preach* from house to house.' There is work enough in a congregation for a minister to do; but nothing renders him more contemptible and despised than a habit of religious gossiping. Let us apply the text.

III. To your general deportment *in the world.*
1. Let your conduct correspond with your preaching. Men will watch you. You may put off the preacher in mixed company; but

---

89 Acts 20:20.

you must never put off the man of God—the Christian. Whatever you may be in the pulpit, if in the world you be frothy, vain, contentious, captious, unfeeling, unjust, or make engagements you cannot fulfil, you will be despised. On the contrary, consistency of character will wear, and live down opposition.

2. Never be ashamed of religion in any company. There is no need to introduce it on all occasions, and in all companies. This would render you despised one way. But be not the subject of cowardly timidity. That would render you equally, if not more, despicable. There is nothing in true religion but what admits of a rational defence. There wants nothing to defend religion but firmness of mind. But if you are ashamed of the cause you have espoused, its opponents will heartily despise you.

To conclude. If the contempt of men be such a matter of dread, how much more the contempt of God! Then so conduct yourself that you may not be ashamed, and not be despised, at his coming!

7. Ministers Fellow Labourers with God[90]

'We are labourers together with God' (1 Corinthians 3:9).

My dear brother, in every address of this kind I wish to be understood as assuming no kind of authority whatever; but simply as concurring in the work of the day, and as presenting to the consideration of my brother in the ministry a few observations suited to the occasion.

The words we have selected afford us an important view of the Christian ministry—co-operators with God! Not, indeed, as co-ordinate, but as subordinate. We labour under him. It is not our husbandry, nor our building, but God's; and the design of the apostle was to cut off the vain-glorying in men to which the Corinthians were so addicted, saying, 'I am of Paul, or I am of Apollos, or I am of Cephas.'[91] Yet, it affords a most honourable and animating view of the Christian ministry—fellow labourers with God! I shall consider the passage in two views; viz. as affording us a directory as to the nature of our work, and an encouragement in our performance of it.

I. As affording us *a directory as to the nature of our work.*
Our work is a labour. If any man enter upon the ministry from a desire to live an easy, idle life, he is under a great mistake. He may make such a life of it, but he will not fulfil his work. And let him take heed lest he be rejected at the last: 'Cast ye out the unprofitable servant into outer darkness.'[92] A proper discharge of the Christian ministry must be a labour. This will appear if we consider a few of the principal parts of which it is composed.

1. A leading part of this work consists in our becoming acquainted with the mind of God in his Word. We must 'labour in

---

90 *Complete Works*, I, 491–494.
91 1 Corinthians 1:12.
92 Matthew 25:30.

word and doctrine.'[93] We cannot 'feed the people with knowledge and with understanding',[94] unless we possess them. Truth is a well—full of water, but deep. A mine—rich, but requiring much labour to dig up the precious ore. Such a depth is there in the Word of God, that inspiration itself does not supersede the necessity of close application, Psalm 27:4. We must be perpetually inquiring and searching, 1 Peter 1:10–12. We must 'give ourselves' to the Word of God and prayer.[95] The very angels are perpetually Gospel students, 'desiring to look into' the things that are revealed.[96] Unless we labour in this way, there can be no proper food or variety in our preaching. 'Meditate on these things: give thyself wholly to them.'[97] The truths of God's word are worthy of being our meat and drink. Digging in these mines is very pleasant work when we can enter into them. But there are seasons when it is otherwise; and yet we must go on, though we scarcely know how; this is labour.

2. Another part is communicating the mind of God so as to apply it to the cases of the people. It belongs to the work of the ministry to apply truth to the circumstances and consciences of the hearers, as well as to teach it; and, in order to this, we must study men as well as things. We must trace the workings of a depraved heart, in order to detect its shiftings and subterfuges—the doubts and difficulties of a desponding heart, in order to remove them, and to point out the way of life—and the general operations of a gracious heart, in order to distinguish between genuine and spurious religion, lest, while we comfort the real Christian, we should soothe the hypocrite.

For these important purposes, it is necessary that we should avail

---

93 1 Timothy 5:17.
94 Jeremiah 3:15.
95 Acts 6:4.
96 1 Peter 1:12.
97 1 Timothy 4:15.

ourselves of two grand sources of information—experience and observation. That which is derived from these sources is taken from life, and is generally more profitable than that which is copied from even the most judicious writings of men, at second-hand. But all this requires labour. I may add, much of the labour that attends this part of our work arises from the state of those with whom we have to deal, and our want of success. In preaching to sinners, we have to attack the strong holds of Satan—ignorance, prejudice, pride, self-righteousness, hardness of heart, unbelief, and aversion from God. Our work here is like having to dig through a rock of flint—we have much labour, and make slow progress. Sometimes we espy a downcast look and a falling tear, and this inspires courage; but these hopeful appearances often subside. Many a character, of whom we have hoped well for years, is still hanging between God and the world, and we know not what will be the issue. These are the things which occasion those pains of labour of which the apostle speaks: 'My little children, of whom I travail in birth, until Christ be formed in you.'[98]

3. Another part of our ministry consists in following up the work of preaching, by close conversation in our private visits. Paul taught at Ephesus 'from house to house.'[99] It is painful and laborious to a feeling mind to tell persons of their faults, and yet we cannot fulfil our duty without. To introduce personal reflections in public, where no answer can be made, and where the tendency is to expose rather than to reclaim, is mean and unmanly; but it is not so in private; there we must be faithful, and, in order to be faithful, we must be personal. But this is hard work. Ministers, as well as other men, have their feelings. They love peace, and they wish to retain the friendship of their people. But if a minister tell the truth, there is great danger of his being counted an enemy, and treated as such. Faithful reproof, therefore, must be self-denying work. The grand

---

98 Galatians 4:19.
99 Acts 20:20.

secret, I think, to render this part of our work as easy as possible, is to love the souls of the people, and to do everything from pure goodwill, and with a view to their advantage—'speaking the truth in love.'[100] The man that can be offended by such treatment, and leave his place in the house of God, can be no loss to a minister or to a congregation.

4. Another part of our work is presiding in the church in the character of a pastor. And this is labour. Those who preside in a large community find it very difficult to manage amidst such a variety of spirits and tempers; and those who preside in a small one may find it still more difficult, where individuals are of more consequence, and therefore, perhaps, more assuming and litigious. A large church is like a large family, in which there is a necessity for constant labour and continual attention, to keep things in proper order. But a small church may be compared to a little boat, floating on the waters—a single wrong movement may overset it. In either case we had need be endued with righteousness, godliness, faith, love, meekness, patience, and forbearance. The less we have of self-importance and of tenaciousness in carrying a point, and the more of respect and disinterested regard for our brethren, the less labour will it be to us.

Having considered the Christian ministry under the idea of a labour, I may observe that we are further directed as to its nature, by considering ourselves as 'labourers together with God.'

By this we are taught to labour in the same cause and to the same ends as God. God, in all his operations, keeps certain important ends in view, and we must join with him: for example—to glorify his Son—to abase the sinner—to alarm the wicked—to comfort the believer—and we must unite with God in all this. We must habitually exalt the Saviour and humble the pride of man. Our

---

100 Ephesians 4:15.

constant message must be—it shall be well with the righteous, but it shall be ill with the wicked. We must never comfort those whom God would alarm. When God brings a sinner under concern, it is our business to forward the work. If a man tell me he is a great sinner, it is not for me to soothe him, and to persuade him that he sees things in too strong a light; but rather to convince him that he is a much greater sinner than he conceives, and that the heart of man is 'deceitful above all things, and desperately wicked.'[101] The only comfort I am authorised to offer him is, by pointing him to a great Saviour—One who is able to save to the uttermost all that come unto God by him, and who will never cast out any that apply to him for mercy. It is dangerous, as soon as we perceive concern, to smile and tell the party that this is a good sign, and all will soon be well. It is a good symptom, if it be genuine; but if, before we can ascertain the reality of the repentance, we begin to soothe and console the sinner, we shall be in danger of causing him to be satisfied, instead of urging him to an application where alone he ought to take up his rest; and, instead of being labourers together with God, we shall be found to be labouring against him. God calls him to mourning, and weeping, and lamentation; and it is at our peril to comfort him by anything short of an exhibition of the free grace of the Gospel. We proceed,

II. To consider the passage as affording us, not only a directory as to the nature of our work, but *an encouragement in the discharge of it.*

And this is derivable from the latter clause—'labourers together with God.' If we be with God, God is with us; and that is the greatest encouragement we can have. 'Lo! I am with you always, to the end of the world.'[102]

   1. If we be with God, God will be with us to assist its in our

---

101 Jeremiah 17:9.
102 Matthew 28:20.

private labours. There is much in the prayer of the apostle Paul on behalf of Timothy: 'The Lord Jesus Christ be with thy spirit.'[103] It is this that will sweeten our labour. Solomon speaks of a joy in labour, and certainly, of all labour, none is so productive of joy as digging in the mines of everlasting truth—especially when the Lord Jesus is with our spirit.

2. God will be with us in blessing our public labours. Had Moses gone to the rock without God, he might have spoken, and have smitten it, but it would not have cleaved asunder: the rock would have broken the rod, rather than the rod the rock. The same may be said of our labours on the hearts of men. But with God we shall 'do valiantly.'[104] 'The weapons of our warfare are mighty through God.'[105] God, we may be certain, will not labour in vain; and if we labour with him, neither shall we. 'Thanks be to God, who always causeth us to triumph in Christ, and always maketh manifest the savour of his knowledge by us.'[106] My brother, if we be faithful labourers, we shall in no wise lose our reward.

103 2 Timothy 4:22.
104 Psalm 60:12; 108:13.
105 2 Corinthians 10:4.
106 2 Corinthians 2:14.

8. The Nature of the Gospel, and the Manner in which it ought to be Preached[107]

'Praying, for us, that God would open unto us a door of utterance, to speak the mystery of Christ, [...] that I may make it manifest, as I ought to speak' (Colossians 4:3, 4).

My dear brother, I have chosen this passage, on the present occasion, as expressing not the whole of your work, but an important part of it—preaching the gospel. For the discharge of this, an apostle besought the prayers of his brethren, and so should we.

The words imply that, to do justice to the gospel, or to preach it as it ought to be preached, we need a special divine influence, and consequently the prayers of our brethren. I wish at this time to call your attention to the work itself—the manner in which the gospel ought to be preached; and then to offer a few motives to your consideration.

I. I shall call your attention to *the manner in which the Gospel ought to be preached.*

It is not my wish to dismay your spirit, but yet I desire to impress you with a sense of the importance of the work of the ministry, that, like the apostle, you may cry to him who alone can give you strength to discharge it. That we may form some idea of the manner in which the Gospel ought to be preached, it is necessary to consider some of its leading properties. We may mention four or five.

1. The Gospel is a message which implies a disagreeable and heavy charge against those to whom it is addressed, and therefore requires great faithfulness. It supposes that all mankind are the

---

107 *Complete Works*, I, 494–496. The reference in this sermon to taking Samuel Pearce as an example of how to preach the Gospel is an indication that this sermon must have been preached after Pearce's death in 1799.

enemies of God, and exposed to his righteous displeasure. You will have to do with the wicked as well as with the righteous, and you must not flatter them. It is at your peril to say anything soothing to the wicked. It will be very painful to keep them at a distance, and to exhibit to them the threatenings of God's Word against them. They will be trying to shift the blame, and to invent excuses; but you must follow up your charges. Their hearts may rise against you, and they may be displeased with your preaching; but you must not desist.

If we could go with a message of approbation and applause—if we could tell our auditory that they are amiable and virtuous beings, with only a few imperfections, which God will doubtless overlook—it might be much more pleasing and agreeable to ourselves as men. We can feel no pleasure in accusing our species. But woe unto us if we speak not the truth! The wicked will perish, and their blood will be required at our hand! Ezekiel 3:16–21. Then beware of softening matters, either with the unconverted or the backslider. Beware of giving up the authority of God over the heart, and of allowing either that the heartless services of the unconverted are pleasing to him, or if not, that the fault is not in them. Beware of countenancing their own views of themselves, that they are poor pitiable creatures instead of sinners. The wound must be probed, or your patient will be lost! O! if we preach the gospel as we ought to preach it, what fidelity is here required! You must, my brother, side with God against an ungodly world. You must follow the windings of their evil hearts; you must detect them in all their refuges of lies, that they may flee to the only refuge set before them in the gospel. However it may pain you, or offend your hearers, if you would preach the gospel as you ought to preach it— you must be faithful.

2. The Gospel is a message in which we have truth and justice on our side; and therefore we ought to be firm and fearless of

consequences. Speak boldly, Ephesians 6:19–20. If a man's cause be bad, it must render him timid; but to be timid in the cause of God and truth is unworthy. When, however, I recommend boldness, I do not mean that which is opposed to modesty and respectful feeling, nor yet that dogmatical rant which deals in assertion without evidence; but that which is opposed to mercenary fear and cowardice. You must not calculate consequences as they respect this life. If you would preach the Gospel as you ought to preach it, the approbation of God must be your main object. What if you were to lose your friends and diminish your income; nay, what if you lose your liberty, or even your life—what would this all be, compared with the loss of the favour and friendship of God? Woe unto us, if we shun to declare any part of the counsel of God! He that is afraid or ashamed to preach the whole of the gospel, in all its implications and bearings, let him stand aside; he is utterly unworthy of being a soldier of Jesus Christ. Sometimes, if you would speak the whole truth, you may be reproached as unsound and heterodox. But you must not yield to popular clamour. If you have truth on your side, stand firm against all opposition.

3. The Gospel is a message full of importance, and therefore you must be in earnest. If your message respected the health of your hearers, or their temporal interest, or their reputation, it would be thought important. But what are these compared with the salvation of their souls! Salvation by Jesus Christ is God's last remedy—his ultimatum with a lost world, Mark 16:16; Acts 4:12. There remaineth no other sacrifice for sins. Then do not trifle on such subjects as these, lest you lose your own soul. What can be thought of you if you employ your time in making pretty speeches, and turning elegant periods, instead of endeavouring to 'save yourself and them that hear you!'[108] What if, instead of beseeching sinners to be reconciled to God, you should crack jokes before them,

---

108 See 1 Timothy 4:16.

to excite a laugh! What can be thought of you if you trifle with principles, and join the sneer of the poet, when he says,

For modes of faith let graceless zealots fight
He can't be wrong whose life is in the right![109]

Your hearers will doubtless conceive that you are insincere, and that you do not believe the message you are appointed to deliver.

4. The Gospel is a message that abounds with deep wisdom, and therefore we ought to possess a deep insight into it, and to cultivate great plainness of speech. The Gospel is a mystery, and a mystery that requires to be made manifest. A mystery is something hidden, or secret. Such are the great things of God. They are 'hid from the wise and the prudent, and revealed unto babes.'[110] 'Unto you it is given to know the mysteries of the kingdom of God.'[111] Much of it, indeed, was hidden from Old Testament believers, Ephesians 3:5. Nor is it known even to New Testament believers but by the Spirit, 1 Corinthians 2:10.[112] Nor is it fully comprehensible to any; for it is called 'unsearchable riches.'[113] 'Great is the mystery of godliness.'[114] Even angels make it their study. Then to make these things manifest must require great insight into them, and great plainness of speech. Do not be content with superficial views of the Gospel. Read and think for yourself on every subject. Read the Bible, not merely for texts, but for Scriptural knowledge. Truth attained in this way is like property—it will wear the better for having been acquired by dint of industry. To preach the Gospel as we ought to

---

109 Alexander Pope, *Essay on Man: Epistle III—Of the Nature and State of Man with Respect to Society*, lines 304–305.

110 Matthew 11:25.

111 Luke 8:10.

112 Fuller's text has 1 Corinthians 2:7, but he obviously means 1 Corinthians 2:10, since verse 7 does not mention the Spirit, while verse 10 emphasizes the Spirit's revealing power.

113 Ephesians 3:8.

114 1 Timothy 3:16.

preach it requires, not the subtilty of the metaphysician, but the simplicity of the Christian.

5. The Gospel is a message of love, and therefore it ought to be preached with great affection. Never were such messages of love announced to the world before. 'God so loved the world', etc.[115] 'Come ye out from them, be ye separate', etc.[116] This is fitly called 'the glorious Gospel of the blessed God.'[117] It is an overflow of his blessedness. To preach these things with an unfeeling heart is not to preach as we ought to preach. Cultivate the affectionate. Not indeed an affectation of feeling, but genuine feeling. Christ wept over sinners, and so must we. If we trifle with men, or be careless about their salvation, or deal forth damnation with an unfeeling heart, we do not preach as we ought.

II. Let me offer *a few motives* to this duty of preaching the gospel as it ought to be preached.

1. Consider the examples held up for your imitation. You have Peter, Paul, John, in each of whom these things are exemplified. Nay, more, you have Christ. Nor have you examples in distant ages only; but you have seen some, even among you—Pearce![118]

2. Consider the examples exhibited for your warning. Some have sunk into indolence and self-indulgence; sauntering about and gossiping, instead of preaching, from house to house; and there has been an end of them. Some have risen into pride and priestly insolence, and there has been an end of them. Some have trifled with the truth, and God has given them up to destructive error. Others have plunged into political speculations, which have eaten up all their religion: aiming to govern the world, they have lost the government of their own souls, and of their peculiar charge.

---

115 John 3:16.

116 2 Corinthians 6:17.

117 1 Timothy 1:11.

118 Samuel Pearce, whose life Fuller had written. See above, page 82, note 48.

3. Consider the effects that may follow. If you were deputed to negotiate a peace between the contending powers of Europe, you would tremble lest the curses of many should fall upon you. My brother, be faithful, and you shall receive a crown. If you be not, the eternal curse of God awaits you!

9. The Work and Encouragements of the Christian Minister[119]

'His lord said unto him, Well done, thou good and faithful servant: thou hast been faithful over a few things, I will make thee ruler over many things: enter thou into the joy of thy lord.' (Matthew 25:21).

Such is the solemn and important charge, my brother, allotted you, that if you were to contemplate it merely as it relates to its difficulties, you might shrink at the thought of it; but I rejoice to say you enter upon your pastoral work under favourable auspices. You have the hearts of your people; and that point gained is more than a thousand. You could never expect to do them good, unless you were interested in their affections.

I feel a pleasure in complying with your desire that I should address you on the present interesting occasion, and shall request your candid attention to a few observations founded on a part of the parable of the talents.

It is worthy of notice, that, as our Lord approached the close of his ministry, his preaching partook of an increasing solemnity. This chapter concludes his ministerial discourses, and is all upon the subject of the last judgment. The parable of the virgins, and that of the talents, both lead to the same point. And these are followed by a solemn representation of the final judgment. The world is convened, and the Son of God distributes everlasting salvation to his people, and everlasting destruction to his enemies.

Such was the close of our Saviour's ministry; and from one of these representations I shall address you, that you also may be prepared for his second coming.

The occasion of the parable of the talents is given by Luke. He tells us, that when our Saviour came near to Jerusalem, many

---

119 *Complete Works*, I, 496–501.

thought that the kingdom of God should immediately appear. But it was a temporal kingdom that occupied their minds; and, in order to destroy their vain conceits, our Lord described himself under the parabolical form of a certain nobleman, who went into a distant country to receive a kingdom, and delivered his goods to his servants in trust, of which trust, or of the manner in which they had fulfilled it, they were each one to give an account. This was, in effect, saying to his disciples, 'It is true, I am going to receive a kingdom, but not here; and you shall partake of that kingdom, but not yet.' Thus he led them to expect that until his second coming their business was not to amuse or agitate themselves about what post of honour they should occupy, but to bend their attention to a solemn and important trust committed to them.

We may remark here: (1) The talents do not mean grace, but gifts, or things to be improved. Grace is that by which we improve them. One man had a talent, and yet turned out an unprofitable servant. He never had the grace of God in truth, but had a gift or trust imparted to him, for the abuse of which he was finally condemned. (2) These talents are dispensed in different degrees— some have five, some two, and some one. (3) Every man is called to occupy what he has—and must give an account of it—and no more. He that had two talents received the approbation of his lord, just as he who had five.

We may collect, from the whole, the important work of the Christian ministry, and the encouraging motives to a faithful discharge of it.

I. We have an interesting view of *the work of a Christian minister.* You are here represented as a servant—you are required to be a good and faithful servant—and you must not make light of your charge, though it extend only to a few things.

1. You are a servant of God. You are entrusted with a portion of

his property, of the use or abuse of which, another day, you will have to render an account. God has put a talent into your hands, and says, 'Occupy till I come.'[120]

Many things might be mentioned as included in the talents entrusted to you, as time, property, knowledge, influence, opportunity: for all these you must give an account. But we pass over these as common to you and others, and shall confine our attention to those which are peculiar to us as ministers. There are two in particular which constitute our ministerial trust: the Gospel of Christ and the souls of the people.

The Gospel of Christ. This is impressively recommended by Paul to Timothy, in the close of his First Epistle 'O Timothy! (and Paul never dealt in interjections without feeling his subject to be one of vast importance) O Timothy! keep that which is committed to thy trust, avoiding profane and vain babblings, and oppositions of science falsely so called.'[121] The Gospel is a most sacred trust, and you must keep it. Not keep it back, but keep it safe; hold it fast in your mind and your ministry. The best way to hold fast the truth as a minister is to live upon it as a Christian. Attempt to keep it anywhere but in your heart, and it will go. If it be merely in the memory, it is not safe. He that is reasoned into the truth may be reasoned out of it. It is living upon the truth as a Christian that will cause the heart to be established with grace.

The souls of the people. These also are a part of the property committed to your trust, of which you must give an account. You may say, perhaps, 'There's such a one, and such a one—they have attended my ministry; but I have never been able to discover anything in them friendly to the cause of Christ.' But the question which may be addressed to you is, 'Did you warn them? Did you deal faithfully with them?' In a word, 'Did you discharge your

---

120 Luke 19:13.
121 1 Timothy 6:20.

trust?' If you have, your soul shall be delivered, and their blood shall be on their own heads. But if not, though they perish in their iniquity, their blood will be required at your hands. My brother, you must 'watch for souls as those that must give an account.'[122] You may have to allege, with regard to others, 'They would not receive the doctrine I taught; they were always opposing it, always cavilling at it, and have often caused my heart to ache.' But the question for your consideration is, 'Did you teach them in love? Did you bear and forbear with them? If they have gone astray like lost sheep, have you searched after them with a desire to restore them? Did you preach "publicly, and from house to house?" '[123] My brother, let it be your concern to give your account 'with joy, and not with grief.'[124]

2. You are not only a servant of Christ, entrusted with an important charge; but are required to discharge that trust as a 'good and faithful servant.' The term 'good' stands opposed to 'unprofitable.' A good and faithful servant is a profitable servant. True, we cannot profit Christ absolutely, but we may relatively: he has an interest in the world, and we may profit that—a people, and we may profit them: and be will consider everything done to them for his sake as done to him; and thus you may be a profitable servant. It is not enough that you do no harm. It is true, many are injurious; but others, who are not injurious, are cumberers of the ground, and as such are unprofitable, and as such will be cast out. The servant in the parable is not cast out for what he did, but for not doing what he ought to have done. You are to be a 'faithful' servant. Faithfulness is absolutely required of a servant of Christ. You are not required to be successful: your Lord and Master was not very successful; but he was faithful, and so must you be. There is great need of faithfulness. People love that their ministers should

---

122 Hebrews 13:17.
123 Acts 20:20.
124 Hebrews 13:17.

'prophesy smooth things.'[125] They love a flesh-pleasing, flattering doctrine. This may not be true of all, but it is of many. They love preaching that soothes, and that cherishes hope and comfort, and ease and peace, whatever be their character and their state; hence multitudes will tell you that they cannot profit under a preacher, when the whole secret is that they cannot be comforted in their sins. Probably, if the preacher were to comfort them, it must be at the expense of the Gospel; he must preach false doctrine, and cry, 'Peace', when there is no ground for peace. So do not you. They may complain that you do not feed them: well, nor should you: you are not required to feed men's lusts, but their graces. Be faithful.

Still your faithfulness must be tempered with love. There is such a thing as unfeeling fidelity—and preaching at people rather than to them. Our Lord himself, who is a perfect pattern of faithfulness, and was particularly severe against the hypocritical Pharisees, yet wept over sinners, even while denouncing judgments against them. 'Speak the truth in love.'[126]

3. You must not think it beneath you, though your lot should be to take the charge of 'a few things.' I have often thought of this passage in reference to a small people, and these perhaps chiefly poor. I am aware that it is flattering to human vanity to have large congregations, and on some accounts it is also desirable; but should it be otherwise with you, if yours should be only a small congregation, consisting of a few people, and these chiefly poor, and this for many years to come, what then? Just think of the commendation of your Lord, 'Well done, good and faithful servant; forasmuch as thou hast been faithful over a few things, I will make thee ruler over many things: enter thou into the joy of thy Lord.' Is not this enough? And ought we not, as ministers, to be more concerned to execute well that trust which we have than

---

125 See Isaiah 30:10.
126 Ephesians 4:15.

to be always seeking after a larger? I abhor the spirit that shall send for an orator, merely for the purpose of gathering a respectable congregation. A faithful discharge of the trust which God gives us is the way to have that trust increased. Instead of being anxious for a large charge, we have reason to tremble lest we should be found unfaithful in that which we have. There are times in which the spirits of a minister will flag, on account of the fewness of his hearers. The sight of empty pews must prey on his peace and comfort. But be not discouraged; remember that the thinnest assembly is made up of immortal beings, and chiefly perhaps of those who are yet in their sins; and you have an object of greater magnitude within the possibility of your compass than was ever presented to the grasp of an Alexander, a Caesar, or a Buonaparte. The salvation of one soul is of more worth than the temporal salvation of a world—a soul, purchased by the Son of God himself. Think of this, my brother, and be not discouraged, even though you should have comparatively few to hear, unless, indeed, the cause exist in your own deficiency. Be 'faithful over a few things', and you shall eventually be 'ruler over many things.'

I proceed to consider,

II. *The important motives* which are here presented to us for the discharge of our trust.

1. You will receive the approbation of your Lord. Place yourself in idea, my brother, before your Lord and Master, at the last day, and anticipate the joy of receiving his approbation. This is heaven. We should not study to please men so much as to please God. If we please him, we shall please all who love him, and, as to others, they are not on any account worthy of being pleased at the expense of displeasing God. It is doubtless gratifying to receive the 'well done 'of a creature; but this in some cases may arise from ignorance, in others from private friendship; and in some cases men may say, 'well done', when, in the sight of him who judges

the heart, and recognises the springs of action, our work may be ill done. And even if we have done comparatively well, we must not rest satisfied with the approbation of our friends. Many have sat down contented with the plaudits of their hearers, spoiled and ruined. It is the 'well done' at the last day which we should seek, and with which only we should be satisfied. There have been young ministers, of very promising talents, who have been absolutely nursed to death with human applause, and the hopes they inspired blighted and blasted by the flattery of the weak and inconsiderate. The sound of 'well done' has been reiterated in their ears so often, that at last (poor little minds!) they have thought, 'Surely it was well done'; they have inhaled the delicious draught, they have sat down to enjoy it, they have relaxed their efforts, and, after their little hour of popular applause, they have retired behind the scenes, and become of little or no account in the Christian world; and, what is worse, their spirituality has declined, and they have sunk down into a state of desertion, dispiritedness, and inactivity, as regards this world, and of uncertainty, if not of fearful forebodings, as to another. My brother, you may sit down when God says, 'Well done!' for then your trust will be discharged; but it is at your peril that you rest satisfied with anything short of this. Keep that reward in view, and you will not, I trust, be unfaithful in the service of your Lord.

2. Your honour and happiness in the world to come shall be greatly enlarged. If you have been 'a good and faithful servant' here, you shall 'rule' there; and if here you have been faithful over 'a few things', there you shall be a ruler over 'many things.' There will be a glorious augmentation of honour and blessedness. The language is figurative. The idea may be expressed by an allusion to David's worthies, who followed him in his trials, and whom he promoted when he came to the throne; those who, to procure him a little water, fought their way through the opposing army, were highly rewarded. And so Jesus assured his apostles, 'Ye which

have followed me in the regeneration, when the Son of man shall sit in the throne of his glory, ye also shall sit upon twelve thrones, judging the twelve tribes of Israel.'[127]

Of course we are not to understand this literally; but the idea conveyed appears to be this—that a faithful discharge of the trust committed to us in this world will contribute to our honour and blessedness in the world to come. In fact, if this idea is not conveyed, it will be difficult to determine what is.

Nevertheless, the best services we can render are mingled with sin, and therefore, instead of deserving a reward, need forgiveness. The reward we shall receive will be a reward of grace, not of debt. Were it not for the sake of Christ, nothing we do could be accepted, there being so much sin cleaving even to our best services. The Lord accepted Abel and his offering. First he accepts our persons for the sake of Christ, and then our services. And our services, being accepted, become also rewardable for his sake: our future honours are a part of Christ's reward. If you are instrumental in saving a soul, it will be impossible for you to meet that soul in heaven, and not rejoice over it; it will, in fact, be your crown of rejoicing. So your honour and blessedness will form a part of Christ's reward.

It is an unscriptural and irrational notion, that all will have an equal degree of happiness in heaven. All will be perfectly happy, but some will not have so large a capacity for happiness as others. Every vessel will be full, but some vessels will contain more than others. 'One star differeth from another star in glory.'[128] The apostle Paul must enjoy more in heaven than a soul caught up from infancy; since part of the happiness of heaven will consist of remembrance of the past. But the diversity most important for our consideration is that which will arise from the manner in

---

127 Matthew 19:28.
128 1 Corinthians 15:41.

which we have performed our trust. In proportion to the degree of fidelity with which we have discharged the trust committed to us in this world will be the honour and happiness conferred upon us in the next.

3. You will participate in that joy of which your Lord partakes: 'Enter thou into the joy of thy Lord.' You will 'sit down with him on his throne.'[129] Whatever the joy is that was 'set before him', and for which he 'endured the cross, despising the shame',[130] in that joy, if you have 'run with patience the race which is set before you, looking unto him',[131] you shall partake. That which rejoices Christ's heart will rejoice yours: the glory of God in the salvation of sinners. He will not rejoice alone but admit to his joy all those who have had any share in the great work to accomplish which he humbled himself unto death.

My brother, let this thought encourage you amidst all your trials—that you are to enter into the joy of your Lord. 'To him that overcometh will I grant to sit with me in my throne, even as I also overcame, and am set down with my Father in his throne.'[132]

---

129 See Revelation 3:21.
130 Hebrews 12:2.
131 See Hebrews 12:1–2.
132 Revelation 3:21.

Ridley & Holl .sc

Rev.ᵈ Abraham Booth,
London

Pub by Williams & Smith Stationers Court 1, July 1806.

Abraham Booth

10. Preaching Christ[133]

'We preach not ourselves, but Christ Jesus the Lord; and ourselves your servants for Jesus' sake' (2 Corinthians 4:5).

A remark which I once heard from the lips of that great and good man, the late Mr. Abraham Booth, has often recurred to my recollection. 'I fear', said he, 'there will be found a larger proportion of wicked ministers than of any other order of professing Christians!'[134] It did not appear to me at the time, nor has it ever appeared since, that this remark proceeded from a want of charity, but rather from a deep knowledge of the nature of Christianity, and an impartial observation of men and things. It behoves us, not only as professing Christians, but as ministers, to 'examine ourselves, whether we be in the faith.'[135] It certainly is possible, after we have preached to others, that we ourselves should be cast away! I believe it is very common for the personal religion of a minister to be taken for granted; and this may prove a temptation to him to take it for granted too. Ministers, being wholly devoted to the service of God, are supposed to have considerable advantages for spiritual improvement. These they certainly have; and if their minds be spiritual, they may be expected to make greater proficiency in the divine life than their brethren. But it should be remembered, that if they are not spiritual, those things which would otherwise be a help would prove a hinderance. If we study divine subjects merely as ministers, they will produce no salutary effect. We may converse with the most impressive truths, as soldiers and surgeons do with blood, till they cease to

---

133 *Complete Works*, I, 501–504. The mention of death of Abraham Booth (1734–1806) at the beginning of this sermon means that it was preached after 1806.

134 On the life and ministry of Abraham Booth, see Ernest A. Payne, 'Abraham Booth, 1734–1806', *The Baptist Quarterly*, 26 (1975–1976): 28–42; Robert W. Oliver, *From John Spilsbury to Ernest Kevan: The Literary Contribution of London's Oldest Baptist Church* (London: Grace Publications Trust, 1985), 14–17.

135 Cf. 2 Corinthians 13:5.

make any impression upon us. We must meditate on these things as Christians, first feeding our own souls upon them, and then imparting that which we have believed and felt to others; or, whatever good we may do to them, we shall receive none ourselves. Unless we mix faith with what we preach, as well as with what we hear, the word will not profit us. It may be on these accounts that ministers, while employed in watching over others, are so solemnly warned against neglecting themselves: 'Take heed unto yourselves and to all the flock', etc.[136] 'Take heed unto thyself, and unto the doctrine; continue in them; for in doing this thou shalt both save thyself and them that hear thee.'[137]

Preaching the Gospel is not the only work of a Christian minister; but it is a very important part of his duty, and that which, if rightly attended to, will be followed by other things. To this, therefore, I shall request your attention.

You cannot have a better model than that which is here held up to you. The example of the apostles and primitive ministers is for our imitation. Three things are here presented to our notice; what they did not preach—what they did preach—and what they considered themselves.

I. *What the apostles did not preach.* 'We preach not ourselves.'
It might be thought that this negative was almost unnecessary; for, except a few gross impostors, who would ever think of holding up themselves as saviours, instead of Christ? 'Was Paul crucified for you? or were ye baptized into the name of Paul?'[138] Very true, in this gross sense, few men in the present day will be found to preach themselves. But self may be an object of preaching without being expressly avowed, and even while with the tongue Christ is

---

136 Acts 20:28.
137 1 Timothy 4:16.
138 1 Corinthians 1:13.

recommended. And there is little doubt that self is the great end of numbers who engage in the Christian ministry. For example:

1. If worldly advantage be our object, we preach ourselves. It is true there is but little food for this appetite in our congregations. Yet there are cases where it is otherwise. Men have made their fortunes by preaching. And if this have been their object, they have had their reward. If this had not been a possible case, Paul would not have disavowed it as he does: 'Not for a cloak of covetousness, God is witness.'[139]

2. If we make the ministry subservient to a life of ease and indolence, we preach ourselves rather than Christ. We may get but little for our labour, and yet, being fond of a life of sloth (if a life it can be called), it may be more agreeable to us than any other pursuit. It is from this disposition that many ministers have got into the habit of spending a large part of every week in gossiping from house to house; not promoting the spiritual good of the people, but merely indulging themselves in idle talk. I might add, it is from this disposition and practice that a large proportion of the scandals among ministers have arisen. Had there been no danger from these quarters, we should not have met with another of Paul's solemn disavowals: 'Our exhortation was not of uncleanness.'[140] Such a declaration as this was not without meaning. It describes the false teachers of those times, and of all times.

3. If the applause of our hearers be the governing principle of our discourses, we preach ourselves, and not Christ. To be acceptable is necessary to being useful, and an attention to manner with this end in view is very proper; but if the love of fame be our governing principle, our whole ministry will be tainted by it. This subtle poison will penetrate and pervade our exercises, till every one perceives it, and is sickened by it, except ourselves. It will inflate

---

139 1 Thessalonians 2:5.
140 1 Thessalonians 2:3.

our composition in the study, animate our delivery in the pulpit, and condescend to fish for applause when we have retired. It will even induce us to deal in flattering doctrine, dwelling on what are known to be favourite topics, and avoiding those which are otherwise. It is a great matter to be able to join with the apostle in another of his solemn disavowals: 'For neither at any time used we flattering words, as ye know, nor of men sought we glory.'[141]

4. If our aim be to make proselytes to ourselves, or to our party, rather than converts to Christ, we shall be found to have preached ourselves, and not him. We certainly have seen much of this species of zeal in our times—'Men speaking perverse things, to draw away disciples after them.'[142] Nor do I refer merely to men who would be thought singularly evangelical, and even inspired of God, who are continually holding up themselves as the favourites of heaven and the darlings of providence, and denouncing judgments on all who oppose them; and the tenor of whose preaching is to persuade their admirers to consider themselves as the dear children of God, and all who disapprove of them as poor blind creatures, knowing nothing of the Gospel. Of them and their followers I can only say, 'If any man be ignorant, let him be ignorant.'[143] But men who have paid great attention to the Scriptures, and who have preached and written many things on the side of truth, have nevertheless given but too evident proof that the tenor of their labours has been to make proselytes to themselves, or to their party, rather than converts to Christ.

II. *What the apostles did preach.* We preach 'Christ Jesus the Lord.'

This is the grand theme of the Christian ministry. But many have so little of the Christian minister about them, that their sermons

---

141 1 Thessalonians 2:5–6.

142 Acts 20:30.

143 1 Corinthians 14:38.

have scarcely any thing to do with Christ. They are mere moral harangues. And these, forsooth, would fain be thought exclusively the friends of morality and good works! But they know not what good works are, nor do they go the way to promote them. 'This is the work of God, that ye believe on him whom he hath sent.'[144] Preach Christ, or you had better be anything than a preacher. The necessity laid on Paul was not barely to preach, but to preach Christ. 'Woe unto me if I preach not the gospel!'[145] Some are employed in depreciating Christ. But do you honour him. Some who talk much about him, yet do not preach him, and by their habitual deportment prove themselves enemies to his cross. If you preach Christ, you need not fear for want of matter. His person and work are rich in fulness. Every divine attribute is seen in him. All the types prefigure him. The prophecies point to him. Every truth bears relation to him. The law itself must be so explained and enforced as to lead to him. Particularly:

1. Exhibit his divinity and glorious character. The New Testament dwells much on his being the Son of God—equal with God. It was this that heightened the gift of him, John 3:16. Hence the efficacy of his blood, 1 John 1:7. Hence the condescension of his obedience, and the dignity of his priesthood, Hebrews 4:14–16. Hence the greatness of the sin of rejecting him, John 3:18, and of apostasy, Hebrews 10:29.

2. Hold up his atonement and mediation as the only ground of a sinner's hope. It is the work of a Christian minister to beat off self-righteous hope, which is natural to depraved man, and to direct his hearers to the only hope set before them in the Gospel. Be not concerned merely to form the manners of your congregation, but bring them to Christ. That will best form their manners. The apostles had no directions short of this: 'Repent, and believe the

---

144 John 6:29.
145 1 Corinthians 9:16.

gospel.'[146] They never employed themselves in lopping off the branches of sin; but laid the axe to the root. Your business with the sins of mankind is to make use of them to convince your hearers of the corruption of their nature, and their need of a radical cure.

3. Hold up the blessings of his salvation for acceptance, even to the chief of sinners. 'This is a faithful saying, and worthy of all acceptation, that Christ Jesus came into the world to save sinners, of whom I am chief.'[147] The gospel is a feast, and you are to invite guests. You may have many excuses and refusals. But be you concerned to do as your Lord commands. And when you have done your utmost, there will still be room. Dwell on the freeness, and fulness, and all-sufficiency of his grace, and how welcome even the worst of sinners are, who, renouncing all other refuges, flee to him.

4. Preach him as 'the Lord', or Lawgiver, of his church, no less than as a Saviour. Christ's offices must not be divided. Taking his yoke, and learning his spirit, are connected with coming to him. Believers are 'not without law unto God, but under the law to Christ.'[148]

The preaching of Christ will answer every end of preaching. This is the doctrine which God owns to conversion, to the leading of awakened sinners to peace, and to the comfort of true Christians. If the doctrine of the cross be no comfort to us, it is a sign we have no right to comfort. This doctrine is calculated to quicken the indolent, to draw forth every Christian grace, and to recover the backslider. This is the universal remedy for all the moral diseases of all mankind. We proceed to notice,

---

146 Mark 1:15.
147 1 Timothy 1:15.
148 1 Corinthians 9:21.

III. *In what light the apostles considered themselves:* 'Your servants for Jesus' sake.'

Ministers are not the servants of the people in such a sense as implies inferiority, or their having an authority over them. On the contrary, what authority there is, is on the other side: 'Obey them that have the rule over you.'[149] Nor are ministers the servants of the people in such a sense as to be directed by them what to preach. In these respects one is their Master, even Christ. But ministers are the servants of their people, inasmuch as their whole time and powers require to be devoted to their spiritual advantage—to know them, caution, counsel, reprove, instruct, exhort, admonish, encourage, stimulate, pray, and preach. Study to promote their spiritual interests as individuals, and their prosperity as a people.

Nor should ministers think it too much to lay themselves out in this work. They do it 'for Jesus' sake.' This was the motive addressed to Peter. 'Lovest thou me? Feed my sheep. Feed my lambs.'[150] 'Feed the church of God, which he hath purchased with his own blood.'[151] Let Christ be not only the theme of my remaining ministry, but the exaltation of him and the enlargement of his kingdom the great end of my life! If I forget thee, O my Saviour, let my right hand forget; 'if I do not remember thee, let my tongue cleave to the roof of my mouth!'[152]

---

149 Hebrews 13:17.
150 John 21:16, 15.
151 Acts 20:28.
152 Psalm 137:5–6.

11. The Influence of the Presence of Christ on a Minister[153]

'The Lord Jesus Christ be with thy spirit' (2 Timothy 4:22)

In addressing you, my brother, on this interesting portion of Scripture, I shall simply offer a few remarks on the blessing desired, and consider its influence on the discharge of the Christian ministry.

I. Let us offer a few remarks on *the blessing desired.*

If we were addressing ourselves to persons who were strangers to experimental religion, we might despair of being understood on this part of the subject; and even among Christians it is more easily felt than accurately described. We know nothing of Divine influence but by its effects. We know we are created, but we know nothing of creative power. We know we are supported, but we can only feel ourselves upheld. We know Christ promised to be with his servants to the end of the world, and I hope we have felt the effects of it. We feel our wants hitherto supplied, our strength renewed, and our work in some measure succeeded; and we are taught to what to ascribe it. But more particularly,

1. The blessing here desired is something different from gifts. God has favoured you with gifts; but so he did Judas. Many shine and figure away with these, with whose spirits the Lord Jesus Christ holds no communion. Gifts are the gold of the temple; but communion with Christ is that which sanctifieth the gold. Without this, gifts will be injurious both to you and to your people.

2. This blessing is more than grace itself, considered as inherent. I need not tell you that our graces have no separate subsistence. We are the branches living on the Vine. Paul said, 'I live' (and surely he had a right to say so, if any man had!), and yet he checks himself,

---

and adds, 'yet not I, but Christ liveth in me, and the life which I now live in the flesh I live by the faith of the Son of God.'[154]

3. It is a blessing which you shall enjoy in common with your Christian brethren. It is not peculiar to you as a minister, but common to all Christians. And is it the better (you may ask) for this? Yes, it is. The best blessings are those common to Christians, Psalm 27:4; Philippians 3:8. The Romish priests have contrived to secure the cup exclusively to themselves; but it was not so from the beginning: 'Drink ye all of it.'[155] And not only the cup, but the thing signified, is common to all Christians. And the blessings which are common to Christians as such are of the greatest importance to us as ministers. If we study, and pray, and preach merely as ministers, we shall make poor work of it; but if as Christians, we shall prosper. We proceed.

II. To consider *the influence of this blessing on the discharge of the Christian ministry.*

Knowing that without him we could do nothing, our Lord has assured us, 'Lo! I am with you alway, to the end of the world.'[156] And now, by his strengthening us, we can do all things. Observe:

1. It is this that will render the doctrine of Christ familiar to us, and our favourite theme. The Spirit of prophecy is called the 'Spirit of Christ', because it testified of his sufferings, 1 Peter 2:11. And if Christ be with our spirit, though only in an ordinary way, it will lead us to delight in the doctrine of Christ, Ephesians 3:17–18. When Christ dwells in the heart, see what follows! This is the unction by which we know all things. And this is the doctrine which God blesses to the building of his church.

2. It is that which gives a divine energy to our preaching. It

---

154 Galatians 2:20.
155 Matthew 26:27.
156 Matthew 28:20.

imparts a much greater energy than the greatest eloquence, natural or artificial. And though it will not in itself convert sinners, yet God usually honours such preaching. And it is a means of conversion. The apostle 'so spoke that a great multitude believed.'[157] And where such preaching does not convert, it yet commends itself to the conscience. 'They were not able to resist the wisdom and the Spirit by which he (Stephen) spoke.'[158] Apollos, who was 'fervent in the Spirit', by his preaching 'mightily convinced the Jews.'[159] The preaching of Paul was 'not with enticing words of man's wisdom, but in demonstration of the Spirit, and of power.'[160]

3. It is this that will render our visits profitable. It is difficult to turn conversation into a savoury and useful channel. But if the Lord Jesus Christ be with our spirit, all difficulty will vanish. Without this everything will be forced and constrained; and we shall feel especially at a loss in our directions to inquirers.

4. It is this that will sustain your heart under trials. You are aware you must expect these. You will see things in your people towards God that will grieve you. This will enable you to reprove them in love. You will see things in them toward each other that are decidedly wrong. This spirit will cause you to be a peace-maker. You will experience painful things towards yourself: some will not receive your doctrine; some will misconstrue your conduct, and pervert your statements: but if the Lord Jesus Christ be with your spirit, you will not sink under the heaviest trials. You may have to lament your want of success. But go on, and be of good cheer. If the Lord Jesus Christ be with your spirit, though Israel be not gathered, you shall not go unrewarded.

---

157 Acts 14:1.

158 Acts 6:10.

159 Acts 18:25, 28.

160 1 Corinthians 2:4.

12. Habitual Devotedness to the Ministry[161]

'Meditate upon these things; give thyself wholly to them; that thy profiting may appear to all. Take heed unto thyself, and unto the doctrine; continue in them: for in doing this thou shalt both save thyself, and them that hear thee' (1 Timothy 4:15–16).

My dear brother, you will find many things in these epistles worthy of your attention. With a view of showing the connection of the text, let us notice what is said in the preceding verses.

[1 Timothy 4,] Verse 12. Timothy was a young man, and was charged to let no man despise his youth. But how could he prevent that? By being 'an example of the believers, in word, in conversation, in charity, in spirit, in faith, in purity.' Then, whoever might dislike him, no one could despise him.

Verse 13. It is supposed that Paul expected shortly to see Timothy, when he would have many things to say. Meanwhile he directed him how to spend his time to good purpose. In 'reading': God knows all things; but we must receive ere we impart.[162] 'Exhortation': He was not to hide, but to communicate his knowledge of divine things, as he received it; the reading of a minister should be for his people, that he may be furnished with sentiments suited to their cases. Exhortation seems to be that kind of teaching which is from house to house, consisting of counsels, cautions, etc. 'Doctrine': he was to dig in this mine, that he might enrich others.

Verse 14. He was supposed to have a gift, an extraordinary gift, foretold in prophecy, by some of the New Testament prophets, and imparted by the laying on of hands. Yet even this was a talent to be improved, and not neglected. Then how much more ordinary gifts!

---

161 *Complete Works*, I, 506–508.

162 Fuller seems to assume that this means private reading. It actually is an admonition to engage in the public reading of the Scriptures.

Verse 15. This verse expresses how his gift was to be improved. It is a shameful abuse of the doctrine of divine influence to allege it as a reason for neglecting diligent study for the pulpit. Yet such things are; and the advocates of this perversion can quote Scripture for it, as 'Take no thought beforehand what ye shall speak, neither premeditate; but whatsoever shall be given to you in that hour, that speak ye; for it is not ye that speak, but the Holy Ghost.'[163] But this has no application to pulpit exercises, or ordinary ministrations. It was very suitable for the persecuted Christians; for how could they know what to answer, before they were questioned by their persecutors: it was therefore greatly calculated to encourage them, and relieve them from all anxiety. But to apply this direction to our ordinary ministrations is a shameful perversion. See Ecclesiastes 12:9-11.

Give me your attention, my dear brother, while I endeavour to illustrate the different branches of the exhortation of the text, and consider the motives held up to enforce it.

I. Let us endeavour to *illustrate the exhortation.*
The things on which you are called to meditate are what you 'read', the things to which you 'exhort', and the 'doctrine' of Christ. Or on the Scriptures—on the precepts contained in them, and on the doctrines to be deduced from them.

'Meditate on these things.' There is a depth in them that requires it. You may read the Scriptures a hundred times over, and yet be only on the surface, far from having fathomed them. They are able to make us wise, through faith; but to believe without searching argues great indifference, and is building without a foundation. The Scriptures were always considered a deep mine, even when they consisted of only the five Books of Moses. David meditated in the

---

163 Mark 13:11.

law of the Lord 'day and night.'[164] It was to his spiritual growth as water is to a tree.

Do not imagine you understand enough of the Bible; or because you have assented to a few truths, therefore you are in possession of all. Paul desired to know yet more. Angels desire to look into the things revealed there. David intimates that the law contains 'wondrous things',[165] and prays that his mind might be enlightened to comprehend them. A spiritual state of mind is the best expositor, and more is discovered with it, in a few verses, than in whole chapters without it.

Do not be content with general truth. Study the Scriptures minutely, and for yourself, and pray over your study. This will make it your own; and it will be doubly interesting to yourself and your people, than if you adopt it at second hand. Read and think, not merely as a minister, but as a Christian.

'Give yourself wholly to them.' No man can excel in any art or science, but by giving himself wholly to it. Why is it one understands law? Because he gives himself wholly to it. Why is it another understands physic? Because he gives himself wholly to it. Why do rulers understand government? Because 'they attend continually upon this very thing.'[166] And though divine knowledge differs in some things from that which is natural and worldly, yet not in this. It is by constant application and use that our senses discern truth from error, and good from evil, Hebrews 5:14. And you must not only give your whole time to this study, but your whole heart.

'Be thou in them.' It is a shocking thing to be engaged in a work which is against the heart. It is not what we think officially,

---

164 Psalm 1:2.
165 Psalm 119:18.
166 Romans 13:6.

but spontaneously, that proves what we are: not what we do at certain appointed seasons; but the bent of our minds in common, in our leisure hours, when we sit in the house, or walk by the way. Engaging in the work without the heart is the forerunner and cause of many scandals. Time hangs heavy on their hands—they saunter and gossip from place to place—scandalize and listen to scandal—and not seldom terminate their career by impurity.

'Take heed to thyself.' It were an awful thing to guide others to the right way, and not walk in it ourselves. See that all is right between God and your own soul. Public religion, without that which is private and personal, is worse than no religion. We had better be anything than preachers of the Gospel, unless we be personally interested in it.

'And to thy doctrine.' There is great danger of going off from the Gospel—perhaps in submission to great authorities, or to please the people. That minister who makes the taste of his hearers the standard of his preaching may go on, and succeed in pleasing them and himself; but, at the coming of his Lord, it will be said to him, 'Thou hast had thy reward!'

There is also danger of going off from the Gospel by leaning to our own understanding. Consult your own understanding; but remember you are liable to err; therefore do not lean to it, in opposition to the Scriptures.

Finally, 'Continue in these things.' That only is true religion which endures to the end.

II. Let us consider *the motives by which the exhortation is enforced.*

1. Your growth in gifts and graces will be hereby apparent. 'That thy profiting may appear to all.' The meaning is much the same as the parable of the talents: five, by improvement, gaining other five. It holds true in temporal things even, Proverbs 22:29. There

is, however, this difference between their pursuits and yours: they labour to obtain an earthly good; you a heavenly, spiritual, and eternal one. If worldly profit or honour were your object, you might study the embellishments of style, or the arts of the partisan;[167] but if you would be the servant of God, your heart must be in your work. A diligent minister will be a useful one.

2. Your own salvation is involved in it: 'Thou shalt save thyself.' This language does not denote that we are the cause of our own salvation any more than of the salvation of others. But as we may be instrumental in the latter, so we may be active in the former, Acts 2:40. Take refuge in the Saviour you recommend to others. The expression may also have reference to that particular kind of salvation which consists in being delivered from the blood of souls.

3. The salvation of your people may be involved in it. A spiritual, diligent minister is commonly a fruitful one, and a blessing to his people. Consider these exhortations, and the motives by which they are enforced, and may the Lord give you understanding in all things. Thus thou shalt both save thyself and them that hear thee.

---

167 Fuller is using the word 'partisan' in the sense of 'devotee.'

13. Affectionate Concern of a Minister for the Salvation of his Hearers[168]

'We were gentle among you, even as a nurse cherisheth her children: so, being affectionately desirous of you, we were willing to have imparted unto you, not the gospel of God only, but also our own souls, because ye were dear unto us' (1 Thessalonians 2:7–8).

My dear brother, you have requested me to address you on your appointment to the important office of pastor over this people; and I know of nothing more impressive on the subject of the Christian ministry than this whole chapter, both as to what a minister should not be, and as to what he should be. Not of deceit, nor of uncleanness, nor in guile, nor as pleasing men; but gentle, affectionate, laborious, disinterested, holy. Let us, however, confine ourselves to the words we have selected as a text, in which the apostle compares his own ministrations and those of his colleagues to the gentle solicitude of a nurse, whose concern is to impart warmth and strength to her children. 'So we, being affectionately desirous', etc. Three things here require your attention: the feeling of a true minister of Christ towards the people of his charge; the subject-matter of his ministry; and the manner in which he must dispense it.

I. *The feeling of a true minister of Christ towards the people of his charge.*

This is an affectionate concern after their salvation, one of the most important qualifications for the ministry. True, it is not the only one. There are gifts, both natural and acquired, which are necessary, since, without them, we cannot be said to be 'apt to teach.'[169] But this qualification is that without which the greatest gifts, natural and acquired, are nothing as to real usefulness.

---

168 *Complete Works*, I, 508–510.
169 1 Timothy 3:2.

Genius may amuse, but 'love edifieth.'[170] A strong mind and a brilliant imagination may excite their admiration, but this will attract the hearts of the people. Look at the men who have been the most honoured; and you will find that they are not the brightest geniuses, but the humble and affectionate.

Look at the example of Paul. Observe how he felt towards his poor, unbelieving countrymen, who sought his life: 'Brethren, my heart's desire and prayer to God for Israel is, that they may be saved.'[171] Even his zeal for the conversion of the Gentiles bore an aspect towards his brethren after the flesh: 'I speak to you Gentiles, inasmuch as I am the apostle of the Gentiles, I magnify my office; if by any means I may provoke to emulation them which are my flesh, and might save some of them.'[172] He speaks as a humane seaman would in a wreck; who, when he found he could not save all, would do what he could, plunging into the sea and saving at least some of them. Here, my brother, is an example for your imitation, towards the unbelieving part of your hearers.

See also how he felt toward those Christians who had sinned. Witness his Epistles to the Corinthians. How anxious he was to reclaim them! how dissatisfied with anything short of their restoration! Looking upon them as lost children, 2 Corinthians 2; 13:2.

Look at the example of John towards the rising generation. 'I rejoiced greatly that I found of thy children walking in the truth.'[173] And look at the example of our apostle, in connection with the text, towards all to whom he wrote. He could not be satisfied with any reward short of their eternal salvation. All other hope, all other joy connected with them, he considered as of small account; and he

---

170 See 1 Corinthians 8:1.
171 Romans 10:1.
172 Romans 11:13–14.
173 2 John 4.

looked forward to them as constituting the brightest jewels in his future crown.

Most of all, look at the example of your Lord and Saviour. How did the kindness and love of God our Saviour appear! What did he not forego, and do, and suffer! May the love of Christ constrain you!

II. Consider *the subject-matter of his ministry.* 'The Gospel of God.'

1. It is a blessed errand to go on. Good news to a lost world. Angels were visited with wrath, but men with the cup of salvation. There is a pleasure in being an almoner, even of earthly blessings: but you have the unsearchable riches of Christ to impart; you are the herald of peace, and pardon, and reconciliation. How a man, bearing such tidings from an earthly sovereign, would be hailed by a number of convicts!

2. But what is the Gospel? It is not merely the privilege of believers; for then it would not be for every creature. It is a declaration of what Christ has done and suffered, and of the effects; exhibiting a way in which God can be 'just and the justifier of the ungodly.'[174] It is not merely to convince of sin, but also to point to the remedy.

3. Make a point, then, of distinctly and habitually preaching the Gospel. Do not suppose your people are so good, and so well informed, as not to need this. Visit the sick, and you will be astonished how little they know, compared with what it might reasonably be expected they should know. Many sermons are ingenious essays; but if they bear not on this great object, they are not the Gospel. Woe unto you if you preach not the Gospel! Do not suppose I have any particular suspicion that you will not. But

---

174 See Romans 3:26.

I feel the importance of the exhortation, 'Preach the Gospel.'[175] Study the Gospel—what it implies, what it includes, and what consequences it involves. I have heard complaints of some of our young ministers, that though they are not heterodox, yet they are not evangelical; that though they do not propagate error, yet the grand, essential, distinguishing truths of the Gospel do not form the prevailing theme of their discourses.

I love a sermon well laden with Christian doctrine. I love to find young ministers well learned in the Scriptures. Then their preaching will not be dry, but good news and glad tidings. Complaints have been made of some preaching as too doctrinal; and a preference has been manifested for experimental and practical preaching; but that doctrinal preaching which I would recommend should include both. The doctrines of the Scriptures, scripturally stated, are calculated to interest the heart, and to produce genuine evangelical obedience. You need not fear that you shall be limited. You may take a wide range. There is a great variety of subjects which may be introduced; as the purity and spirituality of the law, the evil of sin, the wrath of God against it, and many others: but then all these naturally lead to an explicit declaration of 'the glorious gospel of the blessed God.'[176]

III. Consider *the manner in which a minister should dispense the Gospel*: 'Willingly'; and so as, while imparting the Gospel, to impart their own souls with it.

Some have supposed that it is the matter, and not the manner of preaching, that God blesses. But I see no ground for this distinction. I allow that the matter is of the first importance; but the manner is not of small account. For example: the apostle prays that he might make the Gospel manifest, 'as he ought to speak', Colossians 4:4. And this relates to manner, not to matter. You may

---

175 Mark 16:15.
176 1 Timothy 1:11.

preach even the gospel dryly. It must be preached faithfully, firmly, earnestly, affectionately. The apostle so spoke that many believed. Manner is a means of conveying truth. A cold manner disgraces important truth. 'Willingly.' Where the ministration of the Word is connected with external honours and great temporal advantage, there is no test of this; but where it is attended with self-denial, there is. 'Our own souls.' This is expressive of the deep interest the apostles and their colleagues took in the gospel, and their earnest desire that their hearers should embrace it. Hence we speak of pouring out our souls in prayer. How would you feel in throwing out a rope to a drowning man, or in lighting a fire in a wilderness to attract the attention of one who was dear to you, and who was lost? How did Aaron feel during the plague, when he stood between the dead and the living? O my brother, enter into these feelings. Realize them. Let them inspire you with holy, affectionate zeal. Souls are perishing around you; and though you cannot make an atonement for the people's sins, yet you can publish one, made by our great High Priest; and, receiving and exhibiting this atonement, you may hope to save yourself and them that hear you.

14. Faith in the Gospel a Necessary Prerequisite to Preaching It[177]

'We believe, and therefore speak' (2 Corinthians 4:13).

The words immediately preceding those on which I shall found a few observations on the important work of the ministry are a quotation from the 116th Psalm. David, under his troubles, believed in God, and therefore spoke. And the apostles, under persecutions and reproaches, believed in the gospel, and therefore spoke. They spoke boldly in the name of Jesus, whatever might be the consequence. They might be slain, as Christ was. But then like him, too, they would be raised (2 Corinthians 4:14). If they suffered with him, they would also reign with him.[178]

I shall comprise what I have to offer under two heads of discourse: the subject-matter of the Christian ministry, and the necessity of believing it.

I. The subject-matter of the Christian ministry.

It is that which we have believed. It is of the first importance to a messenger to know his errand. Without this, whatever be our talents, natural or acquired, we are unqualified for the Christian ministry. Without this, the most fascinating eloquence is in danger of becoming an engine of mischief. The subject-matter of the apostle's preaching is variously described: it is called 'the faith',[179] 'the truth',[180] 'the truth as it is in Jesus',[181] 'Christ crucified',[182] 'the

---

177 *Complete Works*, I, 515–518. Fuller gave this address to the students of the Bristol Baptist Academy around 1810.

178 Cf. 2 Timothy 2:12.

179 1 Timothy 3:9; 4:1.

180 2 Timothy 2:18.

181 Ephesians 5:21.

182 1 Corinthians 1:23.

gospel',[183] 'the word of reconciliation',[184] etc. In these descriptions, we see our work.

It does not follow that the dictates of reason and conscience are to be rejected or disused in preaching. The light of nature itself teaches some truth: such as the being of God, the accountableness of man, the fitness of doing to others as we would they should do to us, our being sinners, or what we ought not to be. These are truths which the gospel supposes, and which require to be enforced in subserviency to it.

But several important particulars do follow; as,

1. That we must not deal in curious speculations, which have no foundation in the Scriptures. Some have been turned aside by such an indulgence to false hypotheses, and made shipwreck of faith and a good conscience. A large proportion of the objections to divine truth are of this kind. 'How can a man be born when he is old?'[185] 'How are the dead raised, and with what body?'[186] How can one be three, and three one?; How could Christ be both God and man?; How can the certain efficaciousness of grace consist with free agency and the accountableness of man? Paul would not answer such questions as these by opposing conjecture to conjecture, but in the spirit of the text 'We believe, and therefore speak.'

2. That we must not deal in private impulses or impressions, which have no foundation in the Scriptures. One founds a doctrine on his own experience; but experience ought to be judged by the Bible, not the Bible by experience. 'The prophet that hath a dream, let him tell a dream; and he that hath my word, let him speak my word faithfully. What is the chaff to the wheat? saith the Lord.'[187]

---

183 1 Corinthians 15:1.

184 2 Corinthians 5:19.

185 John 3:4.

186 1 Corinthians 15:35.

187 Jeremiah 23:28.

Another swears that, as God liveth, such a thing is true; but what does this prove, save the impudence and profanity of the preacher?

3. That the person and work of Christ must be the leading theme of our ministry. In this, if we be Christians, we have believed; and this we must preach to others. For example, we must preach him as divine. How else could we know whom we had believed? We must preach him as having assumed our nature, and thereby qualified himself to be our Saviour, Hebrews 2:14–15. We must preach him as dying for our sins, etc., 1 Corinthians 15:1–4. We must preach him as the Saviour of the lost, taking the place of the chief of sinners. We must preach him as the only way of acceptance with God. 'Being justified freely by his grace, we have peace with God, through our Lord Jesus Christ.'[188] In short, he is suited to all our wants. To whom else shall we go? He hath the words of eternal life. So preach Christ.

Every sermon, more or less, should have some relation to Christ, and bear on his person or work. This is the life of all doctrine, and it will be our own fault if it is dry. Do not consider it as one subject among others, but as that which involves all others, and gives them an interest they could not otherwise possess. Preach not only the truth, but all truth, 'as it is in Jesus.'[189] However ingenious our sermons may be, unless they bear on Christ, and lead the mind to Christ, we do not preach the faith of the gospel.

As all doctrinal religion meets here, so does all practical. The Scriptures draw everything from the dying love of Christ. 'Feed the church of God, which he hath purchased with his own blood.'[190] 'Be ye kind one to another, tenderhearted, forgiving one another, even as God for Christ's sake hath forgiven you.'[191] 'Ye know the

---

188 Romans 5:1. The adverb 'freely' is taken from Romans 3:24.
189 Ephesians 4:21.
190 Acts 20:28.
191 Ephesians 4:32.

grace of our Lord Jesus Christ, that though he was rich, yet for your sakes he became poor, that ye through his poverty might be rich.'[192] 'Let this mind be in you which was in our Lord Jesus Christ.'[193] 'Hereby perceive we the love of God, because he laid down his life for us: and we ought to lay down our lives for the brethren.'[194] 'Husbands, love your wives, as Christ also loved the church.'[195]

The same may be said of experience. Christian experience clings to Christ and his gospel. The religion of some, who talk of experience, goes to idolize their own feelings and admire their supposed graces. But true Christian experience thinks little of self, and much of Christ, John 6:68.

II. *The necessity of believing the Gospel* before we preach it: 'We believe, and therefore speak.'

It does not follow that every believer should be a preacher; but every preacher ought to be a believer; for,

1. This is the only motive that will render preaching a delight. How can we discourse on subjects which we do not believe? If we have not tasted the grace of God, we shall feel no pleasure in proclaiming it to others. Is it any wonder that faithless preachers call preaching 'doing duty?' Or that they preach other men's sermons? And that in delivering them they are uninterested by them? But if we speak because we believe, our preaching will be the utterance of a full heart, and our work its own reward. We must taste of truth as Christians, before we preach it. Studying it merely as ministers will never do. Believing belongs to us as Christians.

2. It affords ground to hope for usefulness to others. What effect will the sermons of those ministers have, who, by their frothy

---

192 2 Corinthians 8:9.
193 Philippians 2:5.
194 1 John 3:16.
195 Ephesians 5:25.

conversation, loose deportment, or avaricious spirit, are always counteracting them? The hearers will say, and say truly, 'He does not believe his own doctrine. He may talk of truth, or of holiness and practical religion; but all is vain.' If, on the other hand, we feel and practise what we preach, this must at least recommend it to the conscience; and it often does more. The one resembles a man persuading you to embark on board his vessel, assuring you it is safe, while he himself stands on the shore. The other has embarked himself and all he has; and, like Moses to Hobab, invites you to accompany him.

3. It will render the work of the ministry compatible with common honesty. The world has long accused ministers with being hypocrites. This is malicious enough; but while men engage in this work from indolence, avarice, pride, or any other worldly motive, rather than from the principle expressed in the text, they are furnished with a pretext for such reproaches. If we believe not ere we speak, we only deceive, and the sooner we throw off the deception the better.

4. No other motive will bear the test. What an account will faithless ministers have to give when asked, 'What hast thou to do to declare my statutes, or that thou shouldest take my covenant in thy mouth?'[196] One may have to answer, 'The vanity of my parents led them to educate me for the ministry, and when I grew up I was fit for nothing else.' Another may have to answer, 'My own vanity influenced me: having a taste for learning, and public speaking, and esteeming it a reputable and genteel mode of life, I took to it.' Another may have to say, 'It was my own conceit and arrogance: having a large portion of native effrontery, I made my way, and was caressed by the people.' Oh how different these from the apostles! 'We have believed, and therefore speak.'

---

196 Psalm 50:16.

But why do I thus speak? I am not addressing a society which pretends to train graceless characters for the ministry, or to make men ministers by mere education. They are aware of the necessity of their pupils being believers; and if any of them prove otherwise, they have deceived their patrons. They do not so much as pretend to impart gifts; but merely to improve those which Christ appears to have imparted. They wish to enable the aged and experienced part of our ministers, like Aquila and Priscilla, to expound to the younger brethren the way of the Lord more perfectly.

And as to you, my young brethren, I have no particular jealousy of you; only as we ought to be jealous with a godly jealousy, 'looking lest anyone fail of the grace of God.'[197] You are likely, another day, to occupy stations of much greater importance than if each were a minister of state. Our churches look to you. Many aged ministers are gone. Those that remain will soon follow. God has begun a great work in our day. May you take it up, and carry it on. It is but the other day since we were youths, looking up to those who are now no more. Now the load lies on us. Soon it must lie on you, or on some others. Should you prove yourselves unworthy, God will find others. Deliverance will arise from some other quarter. O men of God, 'Flee youthful lusts, and follow after righteousness, faith, charity, peace, with them that call on the Lord out of a pure heart!'[198]

I ought not to conclude without recommending to the audience that Saviour whom we have believed. We have found rest for our souls. Come ye. Forsake the world and your own righteousness. We have worn his yoke, some of us for forty years, and it has never galled us. Take his yoke, and learn of him, and you shall find rest for your souls. His yoke is easy, and his burden is light.

---

197 Hebrews 12:15.
198 2 Timothy 2:22.

15. The Young Minister Exhorted to Make Full Proof of his Ministry[199]

'But watch thou in all things, endure afflictions, do the work of an evangelist, make full proof of thy ministry. For I am now ready to be offered, and the time of my departure is at hand' (2 Timothy 4:5–6).

Being requested to address a word of exhortation to my younger brethren, I doubt not but I shall be heard with candour and attention; and that not only by those immediately addressed, but by all my younger brethren in the ministry. You will not suppose, then, that I mean to compare myself to an apostle, or you to evangelists; but the work is in substance the same, whether it be in the hands of extraordinary or ordinary men: and as Paul argued the importance of Timothy's work from his own approaching dissolution, I may be allowed to enforce it upon you from kindred considerations; namely, that many of your elder brethren are gone, and others are going the way of all the earth.

You will not expect me, my dear young men, to discourse to you on the advantages of literary acquirements. I might do so indeed, and that from experience. I know the value of such acquirements, both by what I have been enabled to attain, and by the want of that which I have not attained; but it is more congenial with my feelings to speak of things of still greater importance. Three things in particular are suggested by the passage which I have read, and these I shall recommend to your serious attention: namely, the work itself to which you are devoted; the duties inculcated as necessary to the discharge of it; and the considerations by which it is enforced.

---

199 *Complete Works*, I, 518–521. This address was given to the ministerial students at what was known as Stepney Academical Institution in Fuller's day. It was founded in London in 1810. It is now Regent's Park College in Oxford.

I. *The work itself* to which you are devoted.

It is called a 'ministry.' The word signifies, as you are aware, 'service.' The leading character of a minister is that of a servant. This is an idea that you must ever bear in mind. It is a service, however, of a special kind. Every Christian is a servant of Christ, but every Christian is not a minister of the gospel. A deacon is a servant, as the word also signifies; but his service respects temporal things; yours is that on account of which the office of deacon was appointed, that you should 'give yourselves continually to prayer, and to the ministry of the word.'[200] It is that which Jethro assigned to Moses: 'Be thou for the people to God-ward, that thou mayest bring the causes unto God.'[201] Your living under the gospel dispensation renders this a pleasant work; it must, if you enter into the spirit of it, be pleasant to study and impart the gladdening doctrine of salvation.

I have observed two extremes relative to this work; one on the part of ministers themselves, and the other on the part of the people. That on the part of ministers has been an abuse of their office of ruling, a fondness for power, aspiring to the exercise of dominion over their brethren. It has always grated in my ears to hear such language as this: '*My* church', '*my* deacons', etc., as if churches were made for them, rather than they for churches. Do not emulate this empty swell. True greatness will revolt at it. He that will be great, let him be the servant of all. Think of the woe denounced against the idol shepherd: 'The sword shall be upon his arm, and his right eye shall be darkened.'[202] Think especially of him who said, 'I have been amongst you as one that serveth.'[203]

The extreme on the part of the people is this: from the idea of ministers being servants, some of them seem to have imagined

---

200 Acts 6:4.
201 Exodus 18:19.
202 Zechariah 11:17.
203 Cf. Luke 22:27.

that they are their masters. It is true they have a Master, and one to whom they must give account; but it is not to the people of their charge. As Christians, they are accountable to one another, the same as other Christians; but as ministers, to Christ only. In serving the church of God, you will act as a faithful steward towards his lord's family; who renders service to them all, but is accountable to his lord only. Serve the church of Christ for his sake.

II. Let me direct your attention to *the duties inculcated as necessary to the discharge of the ministry.*
These will be found to consist in four things:

1. Vigilance. 'Watch thou in all things.' This is a general quality that is required to run through all our work. If any of you enter the ministry as furnishing you with a genteel post in society, you will be at best a drone, and had better be anything than a preacher. You are watchmen, and must be awake when others are asleep.

2. Patience. 'Endure afflictions.' If you cannot bear these, you had better let the ministry alone. If you be good ministers of Jesus Christ, you will not only be afflicted in common with others, but the afflictions of others will become yours. 'Who is offended, and I burn not?'[204] You must care for all, and expect on some occasions, when you have done, to receive evil for good.

3. Activity in the great work of evangelizing men: 'Do the work of an evangelist.' Without considering you as evangelists in the full import of the term, there is a portion of the work pertaining to that office which is common to us all as ministers. Wherever Providence may station you, my dear young men, be concerned to evangelize your neighbourhood. Look at the situations of a number of the ejected ministers, and see if the

---

204 2 Corinthians 11:29.

effects of their evangelical labours do not remain to this day.[205] Who can look over the churches in Cambridgeshire, without seeing in them the fruits of the labours of Oddy and Holcroft?[206] Who can review those of Bedfordshire, and not perceive in them the effects of the labours of Bunyan, labours for which he suffered twelve years' imprisonment?[207] The same remarks might be made respecting other parts of the kingdom. Emulate these men of God in evangelizing your respective neighbourhoods.

4. Fidelity in discharging your trust: 'Make full proof of thy ministry.' The word means thoroughly to accomplish that which you have undertaken. Such is the import of Colossians 4:17, 'Say to Archippus, Take heed to the ministry which thou hast received in the Lord, that thou fulfil it.' Were you to present a soldier with a sword, and bid him make full proof of it, he could not misunderstand you. Would you see an example, look at that of the great apostle in the context: 'I have fought a good fight, I have

---

205 This is a reference to the Great Ejection of 1662. See above, page 36.

206 Joseph Oddy (1629–1687) and Francis Holcroft (*c.*1629–1693) were both ejected in the early 1660s and became the founders of a number of Congregational churches in Cambridgeshire. For details of their ministries, see H. G. Tibbutt, 'Francis Holcroft', *Transactions of the Congregational Historical Society*, 10 (1969): 295–301; S. Williamson, 'The Oakington Martyrs', *Cambridgeshire Local History Society Bulletin*, 27 (1972): 23–30; Geoffrey F. Nuttall, 'Cambridge Nonconformity 1660–1710: from Holcroft to Hussey', *Journal of the United Reformed Church History Society*, 1, no.9 (April, 1977): 241–258; Margaret Spufford, 'The Dissenting Churches in Cambridgeshire from 1660 to 1770', *The Proceedings of the Cambridgeshire Antiquarian Society*, 61 (1968): 67–95. For help with locating these articles on Oddy and Holcrcoft, the authors are indebted to Mr. Nigel Pibworth of Biggleswade, Bedfordshire.

One of Fuller's paternal ancestors, a Robert Hart of Swaffham Prior, Cambridgeshire, had been converted under the preaching of Holcroft, and two of his maternal ancestors, John and Joan Malden were 'intimate friends' of both Oddy and Holcroft (Andrew Gunton Fuller, *Andrew Fuller* [London: Hodder and Stoughton, 1882], 11–12).

207 This is a reference to the well-known Baptist preacher and author John Bunyan (1628–1688).

finished my course, I have kept the faith.'[208]

But here allow me to be a little more particular. If you would make full proof of your ministry, you must attend:

i. To personal religion. This is often inculcated by the apostle. 'Take heed to yourselves, and to all the flock.'[209] 'Take heed to thyself and to thy doctrine',[210] etc. Many people will take our personal religion for granted, as though a man who teaches others must needs be religious himself; but woe unto us if we reason in this way! Tremble at the idea of being a graceless minister—a character, it is to be feared, not very unfrequent! To what is it owing that some of our churches have been prejudiced against an educated ministry? I may be told, to their ignorance; and in part it is so; but in part it is owing to other causes. The lightness, the vanity, the foppery, and the irreligion of some young men have produced not only this effect, but an

Francis Holcroft

208 2 Timothy 4:7.
209 Acts 20:28.
210 1 Timothy 4:16.

abhorrence of the very worship of God, as by them administered. Who were ever known to be prejudiced against a Pearce, a Francis, or a Beddome, on account of their education?[211] If there were individuals of this description, let them be disregarded as ignorant, and let them be told that vicious characters are found among the uneducated as well as the educated. But be it your concern, my dear young men, to shun these evils. The instructions which you receive, if consecrated to Christ, will be a blessing to you; but if your object be to shine before men, they will be a curse.

ii. Let the time allotted you for education be employed in acquiring a habit of useful study. To make full proof of your ministry, you must give yourselves continually to prayer, and the ministry of the word.[212] 'Meditate on these things, and give yourselves wholly to them';[213] and this to the end of your lives. Let no one imagine that he will leave his present situation fully qualified for the work. If, by prayer and a diligent application to study, you acquire such a habit of close thinking as that on entering the work it shall be your delight to prosecute it, this is all that will be expected of you. It is for the want of this habit of study that

---

211 For Samuel Pearce, see above, page 82. Benjamin Francis (1734–1799) pastored a flourishing Baptist church in Horsley, Gloucestershire. For his life and ministry, see Michael A.G. Haykin, 'Benjamin Francis (1734–1799)' in his ed., *The British Particular Baptists, 1638–1910* (Springfield, MO: Particular Baptist Press, 2000), II, 16–29. Benjamin Beddome (1718–1795) was the pastor of Baptist congregation in Bourton-on-the-Water, Gloucestershire, for over 50 years. See Michael A.G. Haykin, "Benjamin Beddome" in his and Terry Wolever, ed., *The British Particular Baptists. Volume IV. More Biographical Essays of Notable British Particular Baptists* (Springfield, MO: Particular Baptist Press, 2018), 258–273 and Michael A.G. Haykin with Roy M. Paul and Jeongmo Yoo, ed., *Glory to the Three Eternal: Tercentennial Essays on the Life and Writings of Benjamin Beddome (1718–1795)* (Eugene, OR: Wipf and Stock, 2019). All three men studied at Bristol Baptist Academy. It says much for the spiritual vitality of the Particular Baptists of Fuller's day that Fuller can cite three such remarkable pastors as models for emulation.

212 See Acts 6:4.

213 1 Timothy 4:15.

Samuel Pearce A.M

Late Minister of the Gospel

Birmingham.

Pub. Sep.ʳ 1.ˢᵗ 1800. by Button Paternoster Row London.

Samuel Pearce

there are so many saunterers, and have been so many scandals amongst ministers.

iii. In every stage of literary improvement be concerned to have it sanctified and subordinated to God as you go on. On this depends its utility. It were desirable that the study of languages and sciences should commence in early youth, and that religion should come after it to make the last impression, seeing it is this that ordinarily stamps the character. Could we be certain that the faith of Christ, and the gifts suited to the ministry, would follow an early education, this would be our course; but as this cannot be, our dread of an unconverted ministry makes us require religion as the first qualification. Only pursue learning that you may be better able to serve the Lord, and all will be well. It is thus that our brethren in India, though their attainments were not made in the earliest stages of life, have retained their spirituality and increased in usefulness.[214] Let me conclude by noticing:

III. *The consideration with which these exhortations are enforced*: 'For I am now ready to be offered, and the time of my departure is at hand.'

This language denotes an anxiety in the apostle that the work of God might go on when he should have fallen asleep; and if we be worthy of the name of Christian ministers, we must feel a portion of the same. Dear young men, to you we look for successors in the work. It is not for me to say how long your elder brethren may continue; but we have seen stars of no ordinary magnitude set within a few years! It seems but yesterday since they were with us, and we were the juniors amongst them. Now we are obliged to take their place; and you, beloved youths, will soon have to take ours. We do not wish to hold ourselves up as your examples; but the cause in which we have been engaged, and in which the Lord has

---

214 A reference to William Carey (1761–1834) and his two key co-workers at Serampore, William Ward (1769–1823) and Joshua Marshman (1768–1837).

not frowned on our attempts, we do most earnestly recommend to your tender and solicitous regards.

Your elder brethren may be spared a little longer, and yet be able to do but little more. We feel the force of the wise man's counsel; may you feel it too—'Remember now thy Creator in the days of thy youth, while the evil days come not, nor the years draw nigh when thou shalt say, I have no pleasure in them.'[215]

---

215 Ecclesiastes 12:1.

16. Ministers and Churches Exhorted to Serve One Another in Love[216]

'By love serve one another' (Galatians 5:13).

My brethren, having been requested on this solemn occasion to address a word of exhortation to both pastor and people, I have chosen a subject equally suitable for both.

I. I shall begin by addressing a few words to you, my brother, the pastor of this church.

The text expresses your duty: to 'serve' the church; and the manner in which it is to be performed 'in love.' Do not imagine there is anything degrading in the idea of being a servant. Though you are to serve them, and they you, yet neither of you are to be masters of the other. You are fellow servants, and have each 'one Master, even Christ.'[217] It is a service, not of constraint, but of love; like that which your Lord and Master himself yielded. 'I have been among you as one that serveth.'[218] Let the common name of minister remind you of this. The authority you exercise must be invariably directed to the spiritual advantage of the church. You are invested with authority; you are to have the rule over them, in the Lord; but not as a 'lord over God's heritage.'[219] Nor are you invested with this authority to confer dignity on you, or that you may value yourself as a person of consequence; but for the good of the church. This is the end of office: 'Whosoever will be great among you, let him be your minister; and whosoever will be chief among you, let him be your servant. Even as the Son of man came not to be ministered unto, but to minister.'[220] But, more particularly,

---

216 *Complete Works*, I, 544–545. This ordination sermon combined both an address to the ordinand and his congregation.

217 Matthew 23:10.

218 Luke 22:27.

219 1 Peter 5:3.

220 Matthew 20:26–28.

1. You must serve the church of God, by feeding them with the word of life. This is the leading duty of a minister. 'Preach the word; be instant in season, and out of season.'[221] This will be serving them, as it will promote their best interests. For this end you must be familiar with the word. 'Meditate on these things: give thyself wholly to them.'[222] It is considered a fine thing with some to have a black coat, to loiter about all the week, and to stand up to be looked at and admired on the sabbath. But truly this is not to serve the church of God. Be concerned to be 'a scribe well instructed in the things of the kingdom.'[223] Be concerned to have treasures, and to bring them forth. I would advise that one service of every sabbath consist of a well-digested exposition, that your hearers may become Bible Christians. Be concerned to understand and to teach the doctrine of Christianity—'the truth as it is in Jesus.'[224] Be careful, particularly, to be conversant with the doctrine of the cross; if you be right there, you can scarcely be essentially wrong anywhere. Cut off the reproach of dry doctrine, by preaching it feelingly; and of its being inimical to good works, by preaching it practically.

And do all this in love. Your love must be, first, to Christ, or you will not be fitted for your work of feeding the church, John 21:15–17. Also to the truth, or your services will be mischievous, rather than useful. And to Christians, for Christ's sake, Acts 20:28. And to the souls of men, as fellow men and fellow sinners. If love be wanting, preaching will be in vain.

2. You must feed the church of God, by watching over them. 'Be instant in season, and out of season; reprove, rebuke, exhort with all long-suffering and doctrine.'[225] Watch over them, not as

---

221 2 Timothy 4:2.
222 1 Timothy 4:15.
223 Matthew 13:52.
224 Ephesians 4:21.
225 2 Timothy 4:2.

a vulture, to destroy them; but as a good shepherd, who careth for the sheep. If you are compelled to reprove, beware that your reproof be conveyed, not in ill temper, but in love; not to gratify self, but to do your brother good.

3. You must serve them, by leading them on in all spiritual and holy exercises. Lead them by your example. 'Be thou an example of the believers, in word, in conversation, in charity, in spirit, in faith, in purity.'[226] Visit them. You have as much need to pray with them and for them in private, as to preach to them in public. And you must do all this in love. An affectionate example and deportment will draw them on.

II. Let me now address myself to the Church.
You also must serve your pastor, as well as he you, and this in love. You must seek his good, as well as he yours.

1. Be assiduous to make him happy in his mind. If he discharge his work with grief, it will be unprofitable for you. If you be touchy, and soon offended, or cold and distant, it will destroy his happiness. Do not be content with a merely negative respect. Be free, open, kind, inviting to friendly and Christian intercourse and conversation; and be early and constant in your attendance on public worship.

2. Be concerned to render him as easy in his circumstances as possible. If he serve you in spiritual things, is it such a great thing that he partake of your carnal things? I hope he does not covet a haughty independence of you; but neither let him sink into an abject dependence. Worship not with—offer not to God—that which costs you nothing. It is the glory of Dissenting churches, if they voluntarily make sacrifices for the maintenance of the true religion among them.

---

226 1 Timothy 4:12.

3. If there be any thing apparently wrong in his conduct or his preaching, do not spread it abroad, but tell him of it alone. You may have mistaken him, and this will give him an opportunity of explaining, or, if he be in fault, this will give him an opportunity of correcting himself.

And do everything in love. Love will dictate what is proper on most occasions. It will do more than a thousand rules; and all rules without it are nothing.

To the deacons let me say, Be you helpers in everything— whether agreeable or disagreeable.

To the congregation generally, I would say, 'You also have an interest in the proceedings of this day. My brother considers you as part of his charge. His appointment by the church is with your approbation. He will seek the good of you and your children. Then teach them to respect and love him.'

17. Ministerial and Christian Communion[227]

'That I may be comforted with you by the mutual faith both of you and me' (Romans 1:12).

The communion of saints was thought of such importance among the early Christians as to become an article of faith;[228] and where the spirit of it is preserved, it is a charming part of the Christian religion. The text gives us a brief description of it. Paul longed to see the Roman Christians, of whom as yet he had only heard, that he might impart to them some spiritual gift, that they might be established. His faith would comfort them, and theirs would comfort him.

We are here naturally led to inquire what there is in the faith of a minister to comfort Christians—what there is in the faith of private Christians to comfort ministers—and what there is in the common faith of both to comfort each other.

Let us then inquire,

I. *What there is in the faith of ministers to comfort private Christians.*

For when Christians see their ministers, they naturally expect to hear something concerning the faith; and Paul seems to take this for granted. There are three things in the faith of a minister calculated to comfort private Christians:

1. Its being Scriptural and decided. If anti-scriptural, we might comfort the sinner and the hypocrite; if speculative, we might amuse a few ingenious minds; but we could not comfort the Christian. Nor must we be undecided. To see a minister who is decided, on Scriptural grounds, is to see a guide who is well

---

227 *Complete Works*, I, 545–547. Like the previous address, this ordination sermon combined both an address to the pastor being ordained and his congregation.

228 Fuller is referring to a line in the third article of the Apostles Creed that professes belief in the 'communion of saints.'

acquainted with his map, and who knows his map; or a pilot well acquainted with his chart. The reverse will be stumbling and most distressing. If a guide now tells you this is the way, then that, and is at a loss which to choose, it must occasion fear and distrust, instead of comfort.

2. Its being considered, not for themselves only, but as a public trust to be imparted. Paul considered himself a debtor to others; an almoner, possessing the unsearchable riches; 'as poor, yet making many rich.'[229] In fact, the very afflictions of ministers, as well as their consolations, are sent to produce this effect, 2 Corinthians 1:6.

3. Its being a living principle in their own souls, 1 Timothy 4:6. Without this, whatever be our attainments, our ministrations will not ordinarily edify Christians. We must preach from the heart, or we shall seldom, if ever, produce any good in the hearts of our hearers.

II. *What there is in the faith of private Christians to comfort ministers.*

Ministers must receive, as well as impart; and should be concerned to do so, in every visit, and in all their intercourse with their people. Now the faith of Christians contributes to the comfort of ministers, in its being, its growth, and its fruits.

1. It furnishes them with sentiments and feelings in their preaching which nothing else wilt. A believing, spiritual, attentive, affectionate audience, whose souls glisten in their eyes, will produce thoughts in the pulpit which would never have occurred in the study. On the other hand, if a minister perceive in his hearers, and especially in those of whom he should expect better things, unbelief, worldliness, carelessness, or conceit, he is like a ship locked up near the pole.

---

229 2 Corinthians 6:10.

2. In the faith of Christians, ministers see the travail of the Redeemer's soul. And this, if they love him, will be a high source of comfort to them.

3. In the faith of Christians, ministers often see the fruit of their own labours. They often pray for their people, of whom they 'travail in birth' until Christ be formed in them.[230] Such fruit, therefore, of their anxiety and their labour, is very encouraging.

4. The faith of Christians is a pledge of their future salvation. A Christian minister must love his people, and in proportion as he loves them he will feel concerned for their eternal happiness. Well, here is a pledge of it, and this cheers him. Your minister looks around, and feels tenderly attached to you as friends, and as the children of dear friends now with God; and sometimes he enters into the spirit of the apostle, who wished himself accursed, after the manner of Christ, for his brethren, his kinsmen after the flesh.[231] Your faith therefore, as a pledge of eternal glory, must needs comfort him.

III. *What there is, in the common faith of both, to comfort each other.*

Common blessings are best. Let us not desire great things—the wreath of honour, or a crown. Amidst all this, the sweet singer of Israel desired and sought after 'one thing', and that was a common blessing, Psalm 27:4. Extensive attainments, even mental acquisitions, are comparatively poor. An apostle would sacrifice them all for a common blessing—the knowledge of Christ, Philippians 3:8. These blessings are common to the meanest Christian.

1. Its unity. Those who have never seen each other, men of different nations and manners, when they come to converse on Christ and the gospel, presently feel their faith to be one, and love

---

230 Galatians 4:19.
231 See Romans 9:3.

one another; and this is a source of great delight. As a Hindu said of some of the missionaries, newly arrived, 'They cannot talk our language; but we see all our hearts are one: we are united in the death of Christ.'

2. The interesting nature of the truths believed: 'Jesus Christ came into the world to save sinners';[232] 'God manifest in the flesh';[233] 'There is no condemnation to them that are in Christ Jesus';[234] 'He that believeth on him is not condemned.'[235] Christ is come; atonement is made; the way of access to God is opened; our sins are remembered no more; we are no more strangers and foreigners; we live in hope of eternal life. These are things which, if we be in ignorance and unbelief, will have no effect upon us; or if we be in doubt and darkness, like the two disciples going to Emmaus, we shall commune and be sad; but if our faith be in lively exercise, our hearts will burn within us, and time will glide sweetly on.

Learn, from the whole,

1. The necessity of faith to Christian communion. Unbelievers, or, which is the same thing, merely nominal Christians, are non-conductors. Neither ministers, nor others, can receive or impart without faith.

2. The necessity of the communication of faith to profitable visits. We may not always be able to maintain Christian conversation. We are men, and must sometimes converse as such. But Christian visits will be of this kind. It is delightful when they are of this description; and, to promote this, we should avoid large, promiscuous parties.

3. What will heavenly communion be! No darkness; no discord; no carnality; no pride; no imperfection!

---

232 1 Timothy 1:15.
233 1 Timothy 3:16.
234 Romans 8:1.
235 John 3:18.

18. Holding Fast the Gospel[236]

'Hold fast the form of sound words, which thou hast heard of me, in faith and love which is in Christ Jesus' (2 Timothy 1:13).

This epistle was written on the near approach of death, and is very solemn. It is addressed to Timothy, and as such is doubtless especially applicable to ministers; but it is by no means exclusively so, since all Scripture is given for the sake of the Church.

I. Let us notice *the exhortation itself.*

'Hold fast the form of sound words, which thou hast heard of me', etc. The gospel is here denominated 'sound words', and 'a form of sound words'; and requires to be 'held fast in faith and love which is in Christ Jesus.'

1. The gospel is called 'sound words.' Much has been said of sound words, and every one reckons his own creed to be such. I would only observe, that sound words must be true words, and words suited to convey the truth. All other systems are hollow. We must be more concerned about their being true, than fine or harmonious. We must beware of specious words, which are often vehicles of error. The words which the Holy Ghost teaches are the standard of soundness. So much regard as we pay to them, so far are we orthodox, and no further.

2. The gospel is called 'a *form* of sound words.' The word signifies a brief sketch, or first draft; such as artists sketch when they begin a painting. Paul intimates that he had given Timothy such a sketch—a compendium, or epitome. Whether he had given him anything of the kind, different from what we have, we know not; but what he wrote to him and others contains such a form, expressed in different ways. As 'This is a faithful saying, and worthy of all acceptation, that Christ Jesus came into the world to save

---

236 *Complete Works*, I, 547–549. This sermon, like the previous two, combined both an address to the pastor being ordained and his congregation.

sinners.'[237] 'Without controversy, great is the mystery of godliness: God manifest in the flesh, justified in the Spirit, seen of angels, preached unto the Gentiles, believed on in the world, received up into glory.'[238] We have one of the forms in his First Epistle to the Corinthians, chapter 15:1–4. And a still more perfect one in his Epistle to the Romans, chapter 3:24–25.

The term implies two things: (1) That what the apostles taught was a sure guide. We are quite safe here. Where will men go, if the apostles' doctrines are treated as mere opinions? These are the genuine criterion of orthodoxy. Keep within these lines, and you are safe. They are able, through faith, to make you 'wise unto salvation.'[239] By these, the man of God may be 'perfect, thoroughly furnished unto all good works.'[240] (2) It implies that what he taught, though it contained the outline of truth, and as much as was necessary for the present, yet is not the whole. It was only an outline, only a sketch, for Timothy and all other Christians to fill up, and to meditate upon. Paul did not know all. Angels do not. It will require eternity to reveal all. There is plenty of room for meditation; only let us keep within the lines which the apostles have sketched out.

3. The gospel, as a form of sound words, must be 'held fast.' This supposes that we do, at least, hold the faith. Alas! many do not. Some have hold of a wholly false doctrine, and hold it fast too. Some are Gallios, perfectly indifferent, and hold fast the world, or anything rather than the gospel.[241] Nay more, it is to be feared that many who talk and profess much about doctrines, and Scripture doctrines too, yet do not hold them fast. We must find the gospel, as Philip and Nathanael found the Messiah, and then we shall hold

---

237 1 Timothy 1:15.

238 1 Timothy 3:16.

239 2 Timothy 3:15.

240 2 Timothy 3:17.

241 For Gallio, see Acts 18:12–16.

it fast.[242] They sought out Jesus, and compared his character and pretensions with the descriptions of the Messiah in the prophecies; and were convinced from examination. If, instead of being convinced of the truth from actual personal research, we receive the notions of others, without examination, upon their representations, even if these notions should be correct, we shall be in danger of not holding them fast. Many will try to wrest the truth from us. Persecutions—temptations—and false doctrines, sanctioned by fashion and the appearance of learning, have occasionally made sad havoc with the truth, and forced many a one who held it loosely, many a one who received his faith at second-hand, instead of drawing directly from the fountain, and who therefore never fully comprehended it, to give it up.

4. The gospel must be held 'in faith and love.' There is such a thing as a bigoted and blind attachment to doctrines, which will be of no use, even if they be true. The word does not profit, unless it be 'mixed with faith.'[243] And there is such a thing as a sound creed, without charity, or love to God and men. But the gospel must be held in faith and love. The union of genuine orthodoxy and affection constitutes true religion.

II. *Let us enforce the exhortation.*

1. Consider the inestimable value of these sound words. They are the words of eternal life. There is nothing in this world equal to them. They are the pearl of great price.

2. They have been held in such esteem that many of the best of men have sacrificed their lives, rather than part with them. And shall we cowardly desert the truth, or shun the avowal of it, merely lest the indifferent should call us bigots, or infidels, or enthusiasts? There is not a more dangerous foe to the truth than indifference. Then 'hold fast' the form of sound words.

---

242 See John 1:43–51.
243 Hebrews 4:2.

3. They are the only principles that can meet the exigences of perishing sinners. All besides, however plausible, will flatter, and allure, and deceive, and destroy the soul.

4. They are the only source of a holy life. People foolishly discard doctrines under the pretence of exalting practice; but holy doctrine is the source and spring of a holy life. What has the church become where these doctrines are given up? And what have those Dissenters become who have embraced another gospel? Mere men of the world.

5. They are the only source of real happiness. They inspire a peace and joy in health, a cheerful acquiescence under affliction, and a hope in death and the prospect of futurity, to which all are strangers who are building on any other foundation than that laid in the Scriptures by the apostles, even Jesus Christ, himself being the chief corner-stone.[244]

---

244 See Ephesians 2:20.

19. The Pastor's Charge[245]

'Take heed therefore unto yourselves, and to all the flock, over the which the Holy Ghost hath made you overseers, to feed the church of God, which he hath purchased with his own blood' (Acts 20:28)

Consider:

I. The exhortation, viz.
1. Take heed to *yourself.*

2. Take heed to *the flock.*

3. Take heed to *all* the flock.

4. Take heed to the flock to *feed them.*

II. The impressive motives by which it is enforced, viz.
1. You are this day appointed *overseer*, and must one day give account.

2. The flock for whom you are to care, and also to feed, are *the purchase of Christ's blood.*

---

245 This outline of an ordination sermon is taken from Joseph Belcher, ed., *The Last Remains of the Rev. Andrew Fuller* (Philadelphia, PA: American Baptist Publication Society, 1856), 185. It can also be found in John Rippon, *The Baptist Annual Register, for 1801 and 1802* (London, 1802), 858–859. The rendition of this outline in Rippon's *Baptist Annual Register* has been followed in our text.

The sermon was preached at the ordination of Rev. Perkins of Luton Baptist Church, Bedfordshire, on Friday, March 12, 1802. The church's previous pastor, Thomas Pilley (1734–1801) had died the year before. Fuller concluded his sermon by reading the entirety of Paul's address to the Ephesian elders in Acts 20.

Part III: Modern pastoral applications

Chapter 3: A timeless solution

Pastors are leaving the ministry in droves. Recent statistics reveal that 50% of current pastors will not be in the ministry in five years and 80% will not be pastors in ten years.[1] But it does not stop there. Approximately 4,000 churches close every year, with 1,000 of these occurring in my own Southern Baptist context. Needless to say, as evangelicals, we have a major crisis on our hands. There have been many different theories put forth to explain this reality and a wide variety of solutions presented. The tragedy is that many of these so-called 'solutions' compound the problem. Here are two examples.

First is the strategy of pragmatism. Pragmatism is when pastors and church leaders use their own initiative and rely on proven means of growth in secular organizations to do whatever is necessary to accomplish their church growth or attraction goals. Christ and biblical truth no longer become the foundation of building the church. Rather, whatever yields results becomes the main driving force. As you can imagine, this often results in a church built upon entertainment, consumerism, flashy

[1] Bill Gaultiere, "Pastor Stress Statistics" (Soul Shepherding; https://www.soulshepherding.org/pastors-under-stress/; accessed April 30, 2019).

programmes, and shallow spiritual growth. The pastors and church leaders often achieve their goal of attracting many new attendees and members, but is this really satisfying the problem we face as churches?

Second is the strategy of personality leadership. Leadership is a necessary function in any church, but this approach takes the need for healthy balanced leadership to an entirely unhelpful level. This strategy focuses on the leader himself, instead of the leader's ministry of the Word and his care of others. It feeds on the leader's charisma instead of his humble, godly character. This solution relies more on the clever tactics of leadership rather than the leader's gifts and abilities to facilitate faithful, Christ-honoring, biblical ministry and soul care within the church. Consequently, this strategy often creates a CEO-model, top-down structure of leadership that relies too heavily on a certain leader and de-emphasizes the role of gospel ministry being about the care of others and the glory of Christ.

There exists another unfortunate reality as churches attempt to implement these unhelpful strategies. These proposed solutions can crush the soul of the ordinary, faithful pastor who labours in the trenches, trusts in the Lord's timing, and fights to keep his eye on the goal of faithfulness and not numerical growth. These models, and others like them, are not just unbiblical, but they have a tendency to take a man's desire to serve God and fulfil his calling to shepherd souls and lead him to be something he is not—a CEO of a business. When you combine this tendency with the general lack of knowledge and training in self-care that many pastors have, then the burn-out rate cited at the beginning of this chapter should not surprise us.

But there is another way

There is another way to seek to build healthy, vibrant churches that rely on the ministry of the Word, as pastors are freed to 'preach the Word in season and out of season (2 Timothy 4:2).' There is an approach where church members are well cared for both physically and spiritually as pastors are encouraged to 'shepherd the flock among you (1 Peter 5:2)' with the conviction that pastors will 'give an account' to Jesus for every soul under their care (Hebrews 13:17; 1 Peter 5:1–4). There is a timeless solution where a local church is still well-led and organized efficiently without the pastor losing sight of his calling to take heed to himself (Acts 20:28), be a servant like Jesus (Mark 10:43–45), and be an example of that service to his flock (1 Peter 5:3).

To find this 'different approach' and not be lured away by popular modern strategies such as the ones noted above, we should be turning to the Scripture, and then to the examples from the past who have practiced these biblical approaches to pastoral leadership.

Andrew Fuller is one of the finest of these examples. We hope this consideration of Andrew Fuller's personal walk with Christ and the faithful ministry he passed down in these ordination sermons have both encouraged you and challenged you to evaluate your own pastoral ministry in comparison to his example. The aim of this final section is to help you 'connect the dots.' May this summation of the life and ministry of Andrew Fuller funnel down to the modern pastor in these two main imperatives: *Take heed to yourself* and *take heed to your flock.*

Andrew Fuller is not unique in this way. The Apostle Paul summarized the call of a pastor in his final words to the Ephesian elders (pastors) before seeing them for the last time and exhorted them in this way: 'Be on guard for yourselves and for all the flock, among which the Holy Spirit has made you overseers, to shepherd the church of God which he purchased with his own blood' (Acts 20:28). All pastors, including modern pastors, should take note of the two commands—be on guard for yourself and for your flock.

These two imperatives are confirmed in Paul's words to Timothy to 'Pay close attention to yourself and to your teaching' (1 Timothy 4:16) and 'Fulfil your ministry' (2 Timothy 4:5). The imperatives are best accomplished through these pastoral commands of 'Preach the word' (2 Timothy 4:2) and 'Shepherd the flock of God that is among you' (1 Peter 5:2).

One of the many reasons we desired to focus on the ordination sermons of Andrew Fuller is that much like Paul's example to the Ephesian elders, it is the best way for us to know how Fuller exhorted pastors in his day. By implication, we can assume this is how Fuller would plead with called men of God today. There is a weightiness to the words of a seasoned, faithful pastor who stands before a congregation and exhorts their newly called pastor as to what God expects from him as he now shepherds *this* flock on behalf of the Chief Shepherd (1 Peter 5:1–4). Thus, there is a weightiness to the words of Andrew Fuller in this regard, words that are particularly relevant for the modern pastor.

Chapter 4: Take heed to yourself

In many ways, pastoral ministry has not changed throughout the generations. One similarity between Fuller's day and the modern day is the compulsion of pastors to pour out constantly for others at the neglect of themselves. In an amazing irony, pastors rigorously spend themselves to care for the souls of others, while crushing their own soul in the process. This often causes a pastor to neglect his own personal walk with the Lord before being tempted to look to the world's wisdom on ministry methodology. Fuller understood these implications well, and that is why his central message to newly appointed pastors in their public commissioning service was to take heed to yourself.

There are five key areas taken from Fuller's exhortations which would be of great benefit to every modern pastor.

Understand your calling

Pastors often mistakenly identify *pastoral work* as the core of their calling from God, failing to understand that the core of their calling should be their own *personal walk* with the Lord. Fuller understood that to be an effective and faithful pastor a man needs to be closely, deeply, and intimately loving Jesus whilst walking with him daily. A pastor must first feed upon the Word of God for his own soul before being useful as a shepherd who is then equipped to feed it to others. Fuller exhorted a congregation in regard to their new pastor in this way:

> The things which he urges upon you are equally binding upon himself. When he exhibits to you the only name given under heaven, among men, by which you can be saved, and charges you, on pain of eternal damnation, not to neglect it, remember his own soul also is at stake. And, when he exhorts and warns you, if he himself should privately pursue a contrary course, he seals his own destruction.[1]

A reasonable explanation of the pastoral burnout rate and the slide from biblical faithfulness in pastoral ministry in the modern age is *sometimes* the pastor's failure to walk with Jesus. A pastor neglects to feast himself on the word of life he preaches every week. Fuller warns of this:

> We may converse with the most impressive truths, as soldiers and surgeons do with blood, till they cease to make any impression upon us. We must meditate on these things as Christians, first feeding our own souls upon them, and then imparting that which we have believed and felt to others; or, whatever good we may do to them, we shall receive none ourselves. Unless we mix faith with what we preach, as well as with what we hear, the word will not profit us.[2]

Our calling is first to walk with God, pursue personal holiness, feed on God's word ourselves, and experience the sweet presence of Christ as a balm to our own souls. It is in understanding this aspect of our calling that we find the power that God uses to bring fruit from our ministry labours.

---

1 Andrew Fuller, *The Obedience of Churches to their Pastors Explained and Enforced* (*Complete Works*, I, 198).

2 Andrew Fuller, *Preaching Christ* (*Complete Works*, I, 501; see above, page 161)

Strive for usefulness

There is no shortage of efforts to assess whether or not men are called for ministry. Just do a web search for assessment tools in evaluating the skills and abilities needed to plant a church in North America, and pages upon pages of options emerge. The problem is found in what many of these organizations are judging useful. Most of them are evaluating personality qualities, ability to cast vision, and gifts of entrepreneurship and leadership. There is a place for these kinds of evaluations, but they should not be the driving force in determining the calling and gifts of a man called to pastoral ministry. Fuller's words call the modern pastor to a different task of usefulness and self-awareness. That is, a usefulness that arises from spiritual maturity, zeal for the work, and a love for the people rather than worldly gifts and talents:

> Our want of usefulness is often to be ascribed to our want of spirituality, much oftener than to our want of talents. God has frequently been known to succeed men of inferior abilities, when they have been eminent for holiness, while he has blasted others of much superior talents, when that quality has been wanting. Hundreds of ministers, who, on account of their gifts, have promised to be shining characters, have proved the reverse; and all owing to such things as pride, unwatchfulness, carnality, and levity.[3]

Although they have a place of usefulness in the ministry, the modern pastor would be helped to think less of his organizational, entrepreneurial and leadership skills and more on the call of God to labour diligently at the tasks of prayer, ministry of the word, and the shepherding of souls. Fuller would also add the need to do so with all one's might under the lordship of Christ. The pastor-preacher must know and pursue his duty without deviation

---

3 Andrew Fuller, *The Qualifications and Encouragement of a Faithful Minister Illustrated by the Character and Success of Barnabas* (*Complete Works*, I, 143; see above, page 104).

and distraction—his faith and his life properly joined—for a man filled with the Spirit will know how to behave in every department which he is called to occupy. Fuller calls the modern pastor not to a worldly wisdom of leadership and skill, but to a divine usefulness marked by a closer walk with God. He is to be a man who puts his hand to the plough of ministry and leans into that plough with his full weight behind it so as to be most useful in the hands of his bountiful Master.

Cultivate your affections

There is a significant need for the pastor to read, study, think, and diligently engage his mind for the benefit of the flock. However, one danger of focusing on the development of the mind is that the heart can grow cold. There is a great need for the studious modern pastor to allow Fuller to bring a much-needed balance to the mind and heart of the pastor by urging him to embrace his affections. Preaching is just as much heart-work as it is the mind. Soul-care is more about physical presence and relationship connection than it is about having the right words at the right time. Fuller reminds us where this heart-felt work comes from in the soul of a pastor:

> Perhaps the greatest qualifications, the best instruction, the most useful learning, that any Christian minister can attain, without any disparagement of other kinds of learning, is that which is attained in the school of affliction; it is by this he becomes able to feel, to sympathize, and to speak a word in season to them that are weary.[4]

As Fuller reminds us of the kind providence of God in the suffering of his servants, do not miss his call upon the pastor to be enabled to 'feel and sympathize' because of suffering. And it is in this maturing by the fire of affliction that God stirs our own affections for others. This empowers a pastor to minister out of empathy and compassion, which should culminate when he

---

4 Andrew Fuller, *All Things Working Together for Good* (*Complete Works*, I, 391).

preaches: 'We must preach from the heart, or we shall seldom, if ever, produce any good in the hearts of our hearers.'[5]

Fuller would want the modern pastor to see the necessity of embracing his affections as he preaches. To do so will increase his personal enjoyment of his labours, but also encourages earnestness in what he proclaims:

> How would you feel in throwing out a rope to a drowning man, or in lighting a fire in a wilderness to attract the attention of one who was dear to you, and who was lost? How did Aaron feel during the plague, when he stood between the dead and the living? O my brother, enter into these feelings. Realize them. Let them inspire you with holy, affectionate zeal. Souls are perishing around you; and though you cannot make an atonement for the people's sins, yet you can publish one, made by our great High Priest; and, receiving and exhibiting this atonement, you may hope to save yourself and them that hear you.[6]

Just as in Fuller's day, the modern hearer can distinguish the difference between counterfeit zeal and zeal which comes from the earnest soul of a man. Therefore, let the modern pastor take heed to these wise words and embrace his affections in his public and private ministry.

Pursue faithfulness

Most modern churches overwhelmingly determine success on two criteria—numbers and money—and because of this, the modern pastor is often judged based on his ability to produce numbers in the pews and money for the budget. Even worse, a genuinely-called man of God often feels the pressure to produce in these ways and it can lead to discouragement, disenchantment, and

---

5 Andrew Fuller, *Ministerial and Christian Communion* (*Complete Works*, I, 546; see above, page 201).

6 Andrew Fuller, *Affectionate Concern of a Minister for the Salvation of his Hearers* (*Complete Works*, I, 510; see above, page 180).

even a compromise of ministerial convictions. Fuller brings some important clarity to a pastor's call to be faithful, not successful:

> Faithfulness is absolutely required of a servant of Christ. You are not required to be *successful*: your Lord and Master was not very successful; but he was faithful, and so must you be.[7]

These words of Fuller are stunning for the modern pastor, for though they were written over two hundred years ago, they powerfully pierce the fallacy of modern ministry success that pervades our day. Success in ministry has nothing to do with numbers. Besides, ministry is not about success. It is about faithfulness. The temptation to yield to pragmatism or rely on a large personality is so often the result of immense pressure a pastor feels from the culture to not appear like a failure. But God is not impressed with numbers nor how much money a church receives. Modern pastors who take to heart Fuller's reminder that our call is not to success in ministry, but faithfulness, will discover a peace within their labours that will be absent in the vain pursuit of numbers and money.

Focus on Christ

It is essential for a pastor to walk with Jesus every day; out of the overflow of this intimate communion, we can then minister God's grace to others. In our modern, technological, social-media-frenzied world, the foundational simplicity of being Christ-centred in all of our ministry is often overlooked. Fuller reminds the modern pastor of this when he asserts:

> The preaching of Christ will answer every end of preaching. This is the doctrine which God owns to conversion, to the leading of awakened sinners to peace, and to the comfort of true Christians. If the doctrine of the cross be no comfort to us, it is a sign we have

---

7 Andrew Fuller, *The Work and Encouragements of the Christian Minister* (*Complete Works*, I, 498; see above, page 154).

no right to comfort. This doctrine is calculated to quicken the indolent, to draw forth every Christian grace, and to recover the backslider. This is the universal remedy for all the moral diseases of all mankind.[8]

The modern pastor is pressured to make much of himself, his church, his platform, and his ministry. In a culture that screams to make much of yourself, Fuller brings a stunning clarity to the modern pastor who has ears to hear. Make much of Christ. Focus on Christ in every aspect of your ministry. This is a call to 'take heed to yourself' for in looking to Christ and focusing on Christ, the pastor will save both himself and his hearers.

---

8 Fuller, *Preaching Christ* (*Complete Works*, I, 504; see above, page 166).

Chapter 5: Take heed to your flock

It is often hard for the modern pastor to fulfil his ministry because of the confusion surrounding the biblical vision for *that* ministry to which Paul is referring. A pastor 'fulfilling his ministry' gets lost so often in the demands on a pastor to meet the expectations of others. There are cultural expectations as well as the expectations of members in the church. Probably the most powerful expectations are the ones that a pastor heaps upon himself. If a man has been wrongfully informed of what it means to fulfil his ministry, it can lead to tremendous casualties both in the church and in the life of a pastor.

The biblical call of a pastor is wrapped up in Paul's exhortation to the elders in Ephesus: 'Take heed to yourself and *the flock*.' The New Testament gives us a very clear understanding of what it means when Paul said, 'Take heed to the flock' and to 'Fulfil your ministry' (Acts 20:28; 2 Timothy 4:5). This pastoral paradigm also informs Peter's exhortation to pastors when he exhorts elders/pastors to be shepherds—to care for God's people. He writes:

Shepherd the flock of God among you, exercising oversight not under compulsion, but voluntarily, according to the will of God; and not for sordid gain, but with eagerness; nor yet as lording it over those allotted to your charge, but proving to be examples to the flock. And when the Chief Shepherd appears, you will receive the unfading crown of glory (1 Peter 5:2–4).

Peter's exhortation to pastors can be summarized in a single sentence: 'Be shepherds of God's flock under your care until the Chief Shepherd appears.' Or as Paul said, 'Take heed to the flock.' Peter is clear about the who, the what, the when, and the how of a pastor's biblical calling.

What? Be shepherds of God's flock.

Who? The flock that is among you and under your care.

How? Not because you must, but because you are willing, as God wants you to be; not pursuing dishonest gain, but eager to serve; not lording it over those entrusted to you, but being examples to the flock.

When? Until the Chief Shepherd, Jesus Christ, returns for his flock placed in your care.

A pastor's true calling, then, is to shepherd the souls of God's people humbly, willingly, and eagerly, and to do all of this on behalf of the Chief Shepherd, Jesus Christ. There is no difference today. Though our modern culture and life differ in many ways in comparison to Peter's first-century world, the basic responsibilities of pastoral ministry remain the same.

With every exhortation from his ordination sermons, Fuller consistently affirms this biblical call of a pastor and reminds us of the nature of this biblical paradigm in five specific areas.

Preach the Word (2 Timothy 4:2)

Hopefully every pastor is familiar with the undeniable imperative of Paul to Timothy to 'Preach the word, be ready in season and out of season; reprove, rebuke, exhort, with great patience and instruction' (2 Timothy 4:2). Much could be gleaned from Fuller's thought on the matter, but the obvious needs to be stated. To 'preach the word' means to know our Bibles well and be dedicated to the Bible as our central focus in what we proclaim:

> Be very conversant with your Bibles. The company we keep, and the books we read, insensibly form us into the same likeness. I love to converse with a Christian, whose mind is imbued with the sentiments of the Scriptures.[1]

Fuller gives direct instruction to a pastor on the method of this task:

> In general, I do not think a minister of Jesus Christ should aim at fine composition for the pulpit. We ought to use sound speech, and good sense; but if we aspire after great elegance of expression, or become very exact in the formation of our periods, though we may amuse and please the ears of a few, we shall not profit the many, and consequently shall not answer the great end of our ministry. Illiterate hearers may be very poor judges of preaching; yet the effect which it produces upon them is the best criterion of its real excellence.[2]

Fuller was committed to the exposition of the Bible. In the modern world where the pastor feels the pressure to produce large amounts of visible fruit quickly in his church, there exists the temptation to preach something else more clever than God's Word. Fuller, however, unflinchingly held that the Bible was the living Word of God, the divine source from whence springs the life of every church and the vitality of every pastor's ministry:

---

1 Andrew Fuller, Letter to Mr. and Mrs. James Chater and Mr. and Mrs. William Robinson, April 5, 1806, cited in John Ryland, *The Work of Faith, the Labour of Love, and the Patience of Hope Illustrated; in the Life and Death of the Reverend Andrew Fuller* (London: Button and Son, 1816), 258.

2 Andrew Fuller, *Thoughts on Preaching* (*Complete Works*, I, 717).

We need not fear exhausting the Bible, or dread a scarcity of divine subjects. If our hearts are but kept in unison with the spirit in which the Bible was written, everything we meet with there will be interesting. The more we read, the more interesting it will appear; and the more we know, the more we shall perceive there is to be known.[3]

The steady diet of many churches in the modern day is topical, shallow—man-centred talks that often 'tickle the ears.' However, Fuller's commitment to 'preach the word' with genuine feeling and conviction needs to recover the pulpit of the modern pastor as 'the leading duty of a minister.'[4]

Care for souls (Hebrews 13:17)

We are not called to count heads and to simply know a little about the people to whom we preach. Pastors are called to know, love and give an account to Christ for individual souls. The Apostle Peter exhorts pastors to this very clear task to 'shepherd the flock of God *among you*' and to know this flock so well that we can give an account of them to the Chief Shepherd (1 Peter 5:2–4; Hebrews 13:17). Fuller wholeheartedly affirmed that this is the task of a pastor, namely, to care for souls:

> It is not more necessary for a surgeon or a physician to understand the anatomy of the human body, than it is for ministers to understand what may be called the anatomy of the soul. [...] We need, therefore, to know the root of the disease, and the various ways in which it operates. In order to effect a cure, the knowledge of the disease is indispensable; and in order to attain to this knowledge, we must study the various symptoms by which the disorder may be distinguished. [...] Without [a knowledge of sanctified human nature], we shall be

---

3 Andrew Fuller, *The Qualifications and Encouragement of a Faithful Minister Illustrated by the Character and Success of Barnabas* (*Complete Works*, I, 137; see above, page 92).

4 Fuller, *Ministers and Churches Exhorted to Serve One Another in Love* (*Complete Works*, I, 544; see above, page 197).

unable to trace the work of God in the soul; and unable to fan the gentle flame of divine love in the genuine Christian, and to detect and expose the various counterfeits.[5]

Fuller's careful words remind us that we cannot fulfil our ministry to care for souls if we do not engage our people with a certain depth of soul-precision. Despite this biblical call upon the pastor to care for souls, this conviction often gets lost in the church. Modern pastors become more driven to see numeric growth amongst newcomers rather than the spiritual growth of the regular attendees and members. Modern pastors become infatuated with what is popular and exciting, instead of the grinding, much less glamorous work of caring for the soul. Fuller's words to the newly-ordained pastors in his day need to echo to us and call every pastor today to remember God is not impressed with the same things we are. God is warning the modern pastor to shepherd the flock appointed to him knowing that he will give an account to the Lord Jesus for every soul under his care.

Shepherd your sheep (1 Peter 5:1–4)

One great advantage of having such a large body of Fuller's instruction to pastors is that he does not stop at simply urging us to shepherd souls, but instructs us how to do it. Whether in Fuller's day or our day, many pastors see their ministry and care for the flock from their public perch. But as Fuller describes it, to faithfully shepherd a flock has many private ministry implications also:

[V]isiting is an essential part of your work, that you may become acquainted with the circumstances, the spiritual necessities of your people. They will be able to impart their feelings freely and unreservedly; and you will be able to administer the appropriate counsel to much better purpose than you possibly can from the pulpit,

---

5 Andrew Fuller, *Spiritual Knowledge and Love Necessary for the Ministry* (*Complete Works*, I, 480; see above, pages 113–114).

and with greater particularity than would be becoming in a public address. Only let us burn while we shine. Let a savour of Christ accompany all our instructions. A minister who maintains an upright, affectionate conduct, may say almost anything, in a way of just reproof, without giving offence.[6]

No doubt, the public preaching of God's Word feeds the flock in a powerful and important way. But for a pastor to truly know his flock, and for the flock to feel loved and cared for by the under-shepherd, the reality is that it will predominately happen in private ministry. The modern pastor in many ways has lost the conviction to engage regularly in private ministry. Pastors are so busy 'running the church' they do not realize they are running from crucial ministry that awaits them. Fuller acknowledges that although private ministry is hard work, it is necessary work:

> Another part of our ministry consists in following up the work of preaching, by close conversation in our private visits—Paul taught at Ephesus 'from house to house.' It is painful and laborious to a feeling mind to tell persons of their faults, and yet we cannot fulfil our duty without. To introduce personal reflections in public, where no answer can be made, and where the tendency is to expose rather than to reclaim, is mean and unmanly; but it is not so in private; there we must be faithful, and, in order to be faithful, we must be personal. But this is hard work.[7]

This private, personal ministry is hard work. One clear evidence of this is the way many younger pastors today run from what are arguably two of the most important places where private ministry occurs—the hospital room and the funeral home. Busyness and fear seem to be two of the most common hurdles causing pastors

---

6 Fuller, *Spiritual Knowledge and Love Necessary* (*Complete Works*, I, 481; see above, page 116).

7 Andrew Fuller, *Ministers Fellow Labourers with God* (*Complete Works*, I, 492; see above, page 141).

to fail in seizing these golden, God-given opportunities to care for souls and shepherd the flock well. It is in the reality of sickness and death where every human being can no longer deceive themselves of what awaits every sinner born into a fallen world. These two places confront every soul with the frailty of humanity and the reality of death. They force every human being to consider who they are before God. Some of the most significant and fruitful ministry comes in private visits to the hospital, the funeral home, the widow's home, the coffee shop with the faint-hearted, or the living room of the downcast.

Fuller realized an essential insight for soul care—the power of presence. Pastors mistakenly believe the greater impact will be in the many words of shared wisdom they share. However, on many occasions, it is simply their presence in the home of a discouraged soul; that is where God ministers through them in a most sweet and powerful way. It is through the presence of a loving pastor that the sheep will be most inclined to receive words of truth from his lips.

Be a godly example (1 Timothy 4; Hebrews 13:7)

The modern pastoral personality culture has cultivated churches which are built more and more on a single person. It is stunning how much a dynamic preacher or charismatic leader who draws a crowd can hypnotize a congregation to overlook clear carnal practices in his life and ministry. The apostate or immoral fall of a pastor is nothing new. The modern church is reaping what it has sown—a pastoral personality culture that often results in a deeply unfortunate outcome: the fall of pastors.

But the New Testament has no shortage of commands around the pastoral call to be an example of godliness to those entrusted to their care. Paul lists specific qualifications that must be evident in a pastor's life to even qualify for the noble work to which he feels called (1 Timothy 3:1–7). Peter calls pastors to shepherd the flock in such a way that they may prove 'to be an example to the flock' (1 Peter 5:3). The writer of Hebrews exhorts the believers receiving that letter to 'remember those who led you, who spoke the word of God to you; and considering the result of their conduct, imitate their faith' (Hebrews 13:7). Just in case the younger modern pastor might feel he is exempt from this standard of life, Paul wrote this to his young protégé in the ministry, Timothy: 'Let no one look down on your youthfulness, but rather in speech, conduct, love, faith, and purity, show yourself an example of those who believe' (1 Timothy 4:12).

Andrew Fuller spent a great deal of his ordination sermons to those entering their new pastorates with these biblical exhortations on his lips. Here's one example as Fuller references Paul's language in 1 Thessalonians 2, which,

> exhibits him and his brethren as bold in proclaiming the gospel; sincere in their doctrine; acting as in the sight of God; faithful to their trust, and to the souls of their hearers; unostentatious; gentle and affectionate; disinterested; and consistent in their deportment, not only among unbelievers, where even hypocrites will preserve appearances, but also among the people of their charge.[8]

Fuller makes it clear that the example that pastors are to emulate for their people is a clear call from the New Testament. Here are those biblical exhortations in Fuller's words:

> The apostle Paul, in writing to Timothy, is very particular as to personal religion, in a bishop, or pastor. 'Take heed to thyself, and to the doctrine.'[9] 'Keep thyself pure.'[10] 'Be thou an example of the believers, in word, in conversation, in charity, in spirit, in faith, in purity.'[11] Observe, too, the connection in which this exhortation

---

8 Andrew Fuller, *The Reward of a Faithful Minister* (*Complete Works*, I, 542).
9 1 Timothy 4:16.
10 1 Timothy 5:22.
11 1 Timothy 4:12.

stands. 'Let no man despise thy youth',[12] plainly intimating that a holy example will render even youth respectable. Your Lord and Master both did and taught the will of God.[13]

If Fuller were here today, we believe he would be most troubled by the carnality that exists in the lives of some modern pastors and the reticence of fellow pastors to call them to repentance. He would point to the growing number of pastoral falls and implosions as having its root in the lack of humble, godly leadership. He would remind modern pastors first to 'take heed to themselves' so they are equipped to 'prove to be an example to their flock.'

Prioritize your family (I Timothy 3; Hebrews 13:17)

The unique demands and pressures on the modern pastor have led to an inevitable reality—the neglect of the family. As a result, the pastor's family is often imploding. Many modern pastors have lost sight of the fact that an important prerequisite for becoming a pastor as clearly outlined by Paul to Timothy was to be faithful to your wife and shepherd your children well (1 Timothy 3:1–5). When you combine Paul's words of qualification to Timothy (1 Timothy 3:1–5) and link them with the exhortation for pastors to give an account for individual souls (Hebrews 13:17), this profound template emerges: the pastor will give an account for every soul in his family before giving account for any other soul in his flock.

The pastor's wife and children are members of his flock and he must care for them well in order to be qualified to shepherd others. Thus, the pastor is called by God to first care well for his wife and children, before those outside his family. And yet, the modern pastor often functions in the complete opposite. He throws himself into ministry to the detriment of his family. The ones who often sacrifice the most to free him to do the work of ministry—namely,

---

12 1 Timothy 4:12.

13 Andrew Fuller, *On an Intimate and Practical Acquaintance with the Word of God* (*Complete Works*, I, 484–485; see above, page 123).

his family—end up being neglected. A pastor who is not mindful of this all too common dynamic often unknowingly neglects his family under the guise that he is serving God and the church.

Fuller was very aware of this need. It needs to be said that as a result of his numerous responsibilities, Fuller's ministry schedule was complicated. The result of this was that he was frequently away from home. Nevertheless, Fuller was mindful of this call upon the pastor to be present with his family and to be a lasting influence in his home as a man of God:

> If you walk not closely with God there, you will be ill able to work for him elsewhere. You have lately become the head of a family. Whatever charge it shall please God, in the course of your life, to place under your care, I trust it will be your concern to recommend Christ and the Gospel to them, walk circumspectly before them, constantly worship God with them, offer up secret prayer for them, and exercise a proper authority over them.[14]

Fuller was also conscious of the effort this would take for a pastor and understood that the temptation to neglect his family lies in the unique circumstances of the pastor's life. It is a call to minister behind the scenes where most do not see, but requires the utmost care and diligence:

> Attend not only to such duties as fall under the eye of man, but walk with God in your family and in your closet. It will require all your wisdom to bring up your children 'in the nurture and admonition of the Lord.' And if you rule not well in your own house, you cannot expect to maintain a proper influence in the church of God.[15]

As the modern family falls apart in so many ways, Fuller's

---

14 Fuller, *Qualifications and Encouragement* (*Complete Works*, I, 136; see above, page 91).

15 Fuller, *Intimate and Practical Acquaintance* (*Complete Works*, I, 485; see above, page 124).

exhortation to modern pastors to prioritize their family may well lead to a long ministry of fruitfulness. But it will definitely lead to souls well cared for who live under his roof, sleep next to him at night, and look to him for the unique and essential leadership that is God's design for the home.

A concluding word

Paul's most important final words to the Ephesian elders were these: 'Be on guard for yourselves and for all the flock' (Acts 20:28). The pastor's soul, ministry, and family are all wrapped up in those divine words designed to sit on the conscience of every pastor in every age. Fuller did his part. He urged those in his day who would assume this noble calling to take heed to these same life-giving, ministry-guiding words. Let us heed them as well today. Let us die to the modern pragmatic, gimmicky-ministry philosophies of our day that are sure to soon fade away. Let us hold fast to this unchanging biblical approach that will be a joy to the under-shepherd and eternal profit for the sheep (Hebrews 13:17).

In the end, the modern pastor is like Andrew Fuller. Each will stand and give an account for the souls entrusted to them by the Chief Shepherd. Allow this concluding word from Andrew Fuller to a newly-ordained pastor act as a stitch that holds this book of ministry paradigm together:

> My dear brother, permit me to conclude with a word or two of serious advice. First, watch over your own soul, as well as the souls of your people. Do not forget that ministers are peculiarly liable,

while they keep the vineyard of others, to neglect their own. Further, know your own weakness, and depend upon Christ's all-sufficiency. Your work is great, your trials may be many; but let not your heart be discouraged. Remember what was said to the apostle Paul, 'My grace is sufficient for thee, my strength is made perfect in weakness'; and the reflection which he makes upon it, 'When I am weak, then am I strong.'[1] Finally, be often looking to the end of your course, and viewing yourself as giving an account of your stewardship. We must all appear before the judgment-seat of Christ, and give account of the deeds done in the body. Perhaps there is no thought more solemn than this, more suitable to be kept in view in all our undertakings, more awakening in a thoughtless hour, or more cheering to an upright heart. [...] The Lord bless you, and grant that the solemnities of this day may ever be remembered with satisfaction, both by you and your people![2]

---

1 2 Corinthians 12:9–10.

2 Fuller, *Qualifications and Encouragement* (*Complete Works*, I, 144; see above, page 107).

Appendix 1: A letter by Andrew Fuller on pastoral rule[1]

Kettering, August 30, 1810.

My dear friend,

As it is very doubtful whether I shall be able to attend your ordination, you will allow me to fill up the sheet with brotherly counsel.

You are about to enter, my brother, on the solemn work of a pastor; and I heartily wish you God speed. I have seldom engaged in an ordination of late in which I have had to address a younger brother, without thinking of the apostle's words in 2 Timothy 4:5–6, in reference to myself and others, who are going off the stage. 'Make full proof of thy ministry: for I am now ready to be offered, and the time of my departure is at hand!' Your charge at present is small; but if God bless you, it may be expected to increase, and of course your labours and cares will increase with it. If you would preserve spirituality, purity, peace, and good order in the

---

1 This letter is found as Andrew Fuller, 'Counsels to a Young Minister in Prospect of Ordination' (*Complete Works*, III, 497–498). It can also be found in Keith S. Grant, *Andrew Fuller and the Evangelical Renewal of Pastoral Theology*, Studies in Baptist History and Thought, vol.36 (Milton Keynes: Paternoster, 2013), 132–133.

church, you must live near to God yourself, and be diligent to feed the flock of God with evangelical truth. Without these nothing good will be done. Love your brethren, and be familiar with them; not, however, with that kind of familiarity which breeds disrespect, by which some have degraded themselves in the eyes of the people, and invited the opposition of the contentious part of them; but that which will endear your fellowship, and render all your meetings a delight. Never avail yourself of your independence of the people in respect of support to carry matters with a high hand amongst them. Teach them so to conduct themselves as a church, that, if you were to die, they might continue a wise, holy, and understanding people. The great secret of ruling a church is to convince them that you love them, and say and do every thing for their good. Love, however, requires to be mingled with faithfulness, as well as faithfulness with love. Expect to find defects and faults in your members, and give them to expect free and faithful dealing while connected with you; allow them, also, to be free and faithful towards you in return. There will be many faults which they should be taught and encouraged to correct in one another; others will be proper subjects of pastoral admonition; and some must be brought before the church. But do not degrade the dignity of a church by employing it to sit in judgment on the shape of a cap, or a bonnet; or on squabbles between individuals, which had better be healed by the interposition of a common friend. The church should be taught, like a regiment of soldiers, to attend to discipline, when called to it, in a proper spirit; not with ebullitions of anger against an offender, but with fear and trembling, considering themselves, lest they also be tempted. Let no one say to another, 'Overlook my fault today, and I will overlook yours tomorrow', but, rather, 'Deal faithfully with me to-day, and I will deal faithfully with you tomorrow.'

I have always found it good to have an understanding with the deacons upon every case before it is brought before the church.

Neither they nor the members have always been of my opinion; and where this has been the case I have not attempted to carry a measure against them, but have yielded, and this not merely from prudence, but as knowing that others have understanding as well as I, and may therefore be in the right. In this way, I have been pastor of the church which I now serve for nearly thirty years, without a single difference.

A young man, in your circumstances, will have an advantage in beginning a church on a small scale. It will be like cultivating a garden before you undertake a field. You may also form them in many respects to your own mind; but if your mind be not the mind of Christ, it will, after all, be of no use. Labour to form them after Christ's mind, and you will find your own peace and happiness in it.

Mercy and truth attend you and the partner of your cares!

Appendix 2: A letter by Andrew Fuller on pastoral purity[1]

Kettering, November 8, 1810.

My dear young friend,

You have lately put on the harness of the Christian ministry. Mercy and truth be with you! Permit one that is not far from putting it off, to offer a few serious and affectionate counsels relative to the *purity* of your conduct. The number of scandals which have taken place within the last few years, in different religious connections, especially those which have arisen from the misconduct of ministers, is truly affecting. I do not know that such things have occurred in a larger proportion among ministers than among other professors of Christianity, and still less than among irreligious characters; but as more is expected of Christians than of other men, and of ministers than of other Christians, a more than ordinary account is made of their miscarriages.

It is of such things as these that our Saviour speaks in Matt.

---

1 This letter is found in 'Letter from Andrew Fuller', *Christian Watchman* (September 6, 1844): 142.

18:7—"Woe unto the world because of offences! It must needs be that offences come; but woe to that man by whom the offence cometh!" If you examine this impressive passage, you will perceive that the term *offend* does not relate to any thing done by the world, but by the professed friends of Christ; and that not in the way of provoking displeasure, but of giving men occasion to stumble, or be offended with the gospel. The word is σκανδαλον, and denotes a *scandal* brought upon Christ's name by the misconduct of his professed followers, furnishing a handle to the world to continue in sin, and to reject the Saviour. The world is supposed to be seeking occasion to justify themselves in sin, and in the scandals among professing Christians they find what they seek. It is thus that scandals among Christians are a woe to the world; they are so many stumbling-blocks over which they fall and perish.

But if there be a woe upon the world by reason of scandals, there is a heavier woe on "that man by whom the scandal cometh"! The reason manifestly is, that he incurs the blood of souls. The world may stumble at these things and perish; but if our evil conduct has been the occasion of it, their blood will be required at our hands; they have only their own sins to answer for; but we, except we repent and obtain mercy through Jesus Christ, shall have bother our own, and theirs; or rather, theirs will so belong to us as to be a part of our own.

Allow me, my dear young friend, to caution you against certain avenues which lead to these things, especially in the case of ministers, and to suggest a few preservatives against them. A minister must be supposed to possess the respect, esteem, and confidence of his people. Whether they be persons of inferior or superior condition, of his own or of the other sex, he is admitted to a friendly acquaintance with them. Were it otherwise he could have but little hope of doing them good. Yet at this door temptation may enter. If instead of applying the esteem and confidence with which he is treated to their proper use, he be filled with a notion of his own importance, he will soon cease to deserve them. Where self-importance prevails there is but little if any religion; and if this be wanting the worst of evils may be expected to follow. See 2 Peter 2:18 and 19. There may be the greater danger of such a process, if he be called to the ministry from the lower walks of life; so as not to have been formed at an early period to habits of delicacy, honour, and propriety. Being raised in the scale of society, he may be tempted to think himself an extraordinary man, or he would not have been selected and exalted to what he is: and finding himself caressed, it may be, by persons of respectability, of both sexes, who but for his being in the ministry might never have noticed him, he is in the utmost danger, not only from the want of religion, but of a proper knowledge of himself and the world, of being betrayed into unseemly behaviour.

Nor is this all:—whatever may have been his previous station, being a minister, his duty requires him to converse with young persons of both sexes, of the lower as well as the higher orders on religious subjects, such conversations if conducted in a manner becoming the Christian minister, are of great use; but this also is a door at which temptations may enter. If he forget the sacredness of his character; if his conversations with the other sex be private and frequent; if the confidence which is placed in him be employed in gaining an improper ascendancy over unsuspecting innocency; I will not say let *him* beware; but rather let *them* beware of him! Familiarities may originate in Christianity, and yet terminate in infamy. Timothy, though "a man of God," was cautioned to "treat the younger sisters with all purity"—1 Timothy 5:2. It was a rule with the great and excellent John Bunyan, to avoid as much as possible being with one of the other sex alone; shunning not only evil, but "the appearance of evil."

One great preservative against evil of this kind is *a diligent application to reading and study.* It was in an idle hour that David was overcome; and out of those ministers who have in this way dishonoured the name of Christ, the far greater part will be found to be idlers, or persons who have been in the habit of spending the greater part of the week in visiting; not as the apostle did who "taught from house to house," but sauntering away their time in eating and drinking and trifling conversation. It may be said, all ministers have not a capacity for close and constant application; but if so, they ought either to relinquish the ministry, or to fill up their time in some useful employment.

But the greatest of all preservatives is walking with God. If we be "in the fear of the Lord all the day long," we shall be safe, and not else. This is of more account than a thousand rules. Without this, we had better be any thing than ministers. Is there no reason to fear that many of those who have indulged in impure practices are ungodly men? Such we know they were of old who turned the grace of God into lasciviousness. They who "walked after the flesh in the lust of uncleanness," are denominated "cursed children." And though some good men may for a time have been drawn into such evils, yet surely they must have been strangely lost to all just sense of religion ere they could give way to them. Open falls are commonly preceded by secret departures from God, and except we be reprobates, will be followed with bitter lamentations, and sincere return to him.

Finally, whatever of this kind has been permitted to take place in any of our connections, it is designed no doubt to be a warning to us. While we feel a proper abhorrence of the evil, it becomes us to tremble for ourselves. "Let him that thinketh he standeth take heed lest he fall."

I am affectionately yours, etc.

Appendix 3: William Carey's summary of his ordination

William Carey recorded the details of his Leicester ordination for the London Baptist John Rippon, who published it in *The Baptist Annual Register for 1790, 1791, 1792, and part of 1793* (London, 1793). None of the sermons preached on the day appear to be extant.[1]

After I had been a probationer in this place a year and ten months, on the 24th of May 1791, I was solemnly set apart to the office of pastor. About twenty ministers, of different denominations, were witness to the transactions of the day. After. Prayer, Brother [Richard] Hopper, of Nottingham, addressed the congregation upon the nature of an ordination, after which he proposed the usual questions to the church, and required my Confession of Faith; which being delivered, Brother Ryland prayed the ordination prayer, with laying on of hands. Brother [John] Sutcliff delivered a very solemn charge from Acts 6:4, 'But we will give ourselves continually to prayer, and to the ministry of the Word.' And Brother Fuller delivered an excellent

---

1 For Fuller's sermon to the church at Moulton, Northamptonshire, preached on the installation of Carey as their pastor in August of 1787, see *Complete Works*, I, 521–522.

address to the people from Ephesians 5:2, 'Walk in love.' In the evening, Brother Pearce, of Birmingham, preached from Galatians 6:14, 'God forbid that I should glory, save in the cross of our Lord Jesus Christ, by whom the world is crucified unto me, and I unto the world.' The day was a day of pleasure, and I hope of profit to the greatest of the assembly.

Appendix 4: Study Questions on Andrew Fuller, *The Qualifications and Encouragement of a Faithful Minister Illustrated by the Character and Success of Barnabas*

1. What is the importance of examples from Fuller's perspective? How can an example drawn from Scripture be helpful to a young minister like Robert Fawkner?

2. What kind of man was Barnabas? Why is he a good example?

3. What does the epithet "good" in Acts 11:24 mean according to Fuller?

4. How does being a good man work itself out in: (a) the home; (b) one's personal life; (c) one's public life as a minister; and (d) the "general tenor of your behavior"?

5. What is key to making sure "the fire of devotion" does not go out?

6. What does the indwelling of the Holy Spirit entail? According to Fuller, what is meant by the metaphor "full of the Holy Spirit"?

7. What results flow from being filled with the Holy Spirit?

8. Write a small paragraph on the phrase "if we are destitute of the Holy Spirit, we are blind to the loveliness of the divine character."

9. Given the reality of the perseverance of the believer, can a Christian pray David's prayer, "Take not thy Holy Spirit"? If so, why? If not, why not?

10. Explain what Fuller means when he says, "Being full of the Holy Spirit will give a holy tincture to your meditation and preaching."

11. How will being filled with the Holy Spirit impact one's relationship with one's congregation?

12. What is significant about the way that Fuller refers to the members of the congregation whom the minister will visit?

13. How will experiencing the fullness of the Holy Spirit affect one's character?

14. What three possible meanings does Fuller discern in the phrase "full of faith"?

15. What was "the great controversy" of Paul's day?

16. What two extremes does Fuller reject?

17. What does Fuller see as the great temptation of his day?

18. How should a pastor study the Scriptures and why?

19. What "rule" does "Scripture and experience […] confirm"? Discuss Fuller's rule. Do you agree with Fuller? Why or why not?

20. What three distinguishing marks of eminent spirituality or "eminency in grace" does Fuller identify?

21. Identify briefly in one sentence each of the individuals whom Fuller names after "Paul and Peter." What marked their religion of the heart?

22. What three pieces of "serious advice" close this sermon? Is there one of these that is particularly apropos to your life? Explain.

Appendix 5: Other Particular Baptist ordination sermons of the eighteenth century

Beddome, Benjamin. *Ministerial Subordination to Christ* in *Sermons printed from the manuscripts of the late Rev. Benjamin Beddome, A.M. of Bourton-on-the-Water, Gloucestershire.* London: William Ball, 1835; pages 269–273.

——. *The Nature and Authority of the Christian Ministry* in *Sermons printed from the manuscripts of the late Rev. Benjamin Beddome, A.M. of Bourton-on-the-Water, Gloucestershire.* London: William Ball, 1835; pages 302–309.

——. *On the Duty of Ministers to Promote their People's Joy. Delight* in *Sermons printed from the manuscripts of the late Rev. Benjamin Beddome, A.M. of Bourton-on-the-Water, Gloucestershire.* London: William Ball, 1835; pages 356–362.

——. *On the Sources of Ministerial Delight* in *Sermons printed from the manuscripts of the late Rev. Benjamin Beddome, A.M. of Bourton-on-the-Water, Gloucestershire.* London: William Ball, 1835; pages 260–268.

Booth, Abraham. *Pastoral Cautions: An Address to the Late Mr.*

Thomas Hopkins, when Ordained Pastor of the Church of Christ, in Eagle Street, Red Lion Square, July 13, 1785 (London: Button and Son, 1805).

Brine, John. *The Solemn Charge of a Christian Minister considered. A Sermon Preach'd at the Ordination of the Rev^d Mr John Ryland, on the 26th of July, 1750.* London: John Ward, [1750].

———. *Diligence in Study: Recommended to Ministers. In a Sermon, Preached at the Ordination Of the Reverend Mr. Richard Rist, In Harlow, Essex. December 15, 1756.* London: John Ward, George Keith, and John Eynon, 1757.

Crabtree, William. *The Regard which the Churches of Christ Owe to Their Ministers. A Sermon, Preached at the Ordination of The Rev. Joshua Wood, of Halifax, August 6, 1760* in Isaac Mann, *Memoirs of the Late Rev. Wm. Crabtree.* London: Button and Son, 1815; pages 59–115.

Three Discourses Addressed to the Congregation at Maze-Pond, Southwark, on their publick declaration of having chosen Mr. James Dore their pastor, March 25th, 1784. Cambridge: F. Archdeacon, 1784.

Evans, Caleb. *A Charge, etc.* in his and Hugh Evans, *A Charge and Sermon; Delivered at the Ordination of the Rev. Thomas Dunscombe, At Coate, Oxon, August 4th, 1773.* Bristol: W. Pine, T. Cadell, M. Ward, 1773; pages 3–19.

———. *A Sermon, etc.* in Daniel Turner and his *A Charge and Sermon, Delivered at the Ordination of the Rev. Mr. Job David, October 7, 1773, at Frome, Somersetshire.* Bristol: W. Pine, T. Cadell, M. Ward, etc./London: J. Buckland, [1773]; pages 25–40.

Evans, Hugh. *A Sermon, etc.* in Caleb Evans and his *A Charge and Sermon; Delivered at the Ordination of the Rev. Thomas*

Dunscombe, At Coate, Oxon, August 4th, 1773. Bristol: W. Pine, T. Cadell, M. Ward, 1773; pages 21–39.

Fall, Sr., James. *The Charge of God to Feed the Flock of Slaughter. A Sermon Preach'd at the Ordination of the Reverend Mr. James Fall, [Jr.] of Goodman's-Fields, London*. London, 1754; pages 1–21.

Gill, John. *The Work of a Gospel-Minister recommended to Consideration* in his *A Collection of Sermons and Tracts: In Two Volumes*. London: George Keith, 1773; II, 14–29.

——. *The Doctrine of the Cherubim Opened and Explained* in his *A Collection of Sermons and Tracts: In Two Volumes*. London: George Keith, 1773; II, 30–48.

——. *The Form of sound Words to be held fast* in his *A Collection of Sermons and Tracts: In Two Volumes*. London: George Keith, 1773; II, 49–64.

Hall, Sr., Robert. *God's Approbation, the Study of faithful Ministers* in his and Thomas Hull, *God's Approbation, the Study of faithful Ministers—and, The Duty of a People to their Pastor, and one another. Represented in Two Discourses, At the Ordination of Mr. George Moreton, at Kettering. November 20, 1771*. Coventry: J.W. Piercy, 1771; pages 1–38.

Hall, Jr., Robert. *On the Discouragements and Supports of the Christian Minister: A Discourse, Delivered to the Rev. James Robertson, at his Ordination over the Independent Church at Stretton, Warwickshire* [1812] in *The Works of the Rev. Robert Hall, A.M.*, ed. Olinthus Gregory and Joseph Belcher. New York: Harper & Brothers, 1858; I, 127–155.

——. *An Address to the Rev. Eustace Carey, January 19, 1814, On his Designation as a Christian Missionary to India* in *The Works of the Rev. Robert Hall, A.M.*, ed. Olinthus Gregory and Joseph Belcher. New York: Harper & Brothers, 1858; I, 157–176.

————. *The Substance of a Charge, Delivered at the Ordination of the Rev. J. K. Hall, at Kettering, November 8, 1815 [From the notes of the Rev. S. Hillyard, of Bedford]* in *The Works of the Rev. Robert Hall, A.M.*, ed. Olinthus Gregory and Joseph Belcher. New York: Harper & Brothers, 1858; II, 475–483.

Hinton, James. *Duties incumbent on a Christian Church* in John Ryland and his *The Difficulties and Supports of a Gospel Minister; and The Duties incumbent on a Christian Church*. Bristol: Button, 1801; pages 33–53.

Hull, Thomas. *The Duty of a People to their Pastor, and one another* in Robert Hall, Sr. and his *God's Approbation, the Study of faithful Ministers—and, The Duty of a People to their Pastor, and one another. Represented in Two Discourses, At the Ordination of Mr. George Moreton, at Kettering. November 20, 1771*. Coventry: J.W. Piercy, 1771; pages 39–60.

Pearce, Samuel. *The Duty of Churches to Regard Ministers as the Gift of Christ* in John Ryland and his *The Duty of Ministers to be Nursing Fathers to the Church; and the Duty of Churches to Regard Ministers as the Gift of Christ*. London: Button/Worcester: Baskerfield/Birmingham: Belcher/Bristol: James, 1796.

Robinson, Robert. *A Sermon Preached at the Ordination of the Rev. Mr. George Birley, On Wednesday, October 18, 1786, at St. Ives*. [London: Wayland, 1786].

Ryland, John. *The Duty of Ministers to be Nursing Fathers to the Church* in his and Samuel Pearce, *The Duty of Ministers to be Nursing Fathers to the Church; and the Duty of Churches to Regard Ministers as the Gift of Christ*. London: Button/Worcester: Baskerfield/Birmingham: Belcher/Bristol: James, 1796.

————. *The Difficulties and Supports of a Gospel Minister* in his and James Hinton, *The Difficulties and Supports of a Gospel Minister;*

and *The Duties incumbent on a Christian Church.* Bristol: Harris and Bryan, 1801; pages 7–32.

————. *The Difficulties of the Christian Ministry, and the Means of Surmounting Them* in his and Andrew Fuller, *The Difficulties of the Christian Ministry, and the Means of Surmounting Them; with the Obedience of Churches to their Pastors Explained and Enforced.* Birmingham: J. Belcher/London: Button and Son, 1802.

Steadman, William. *The Qualifications Necessary for the Discharge of the Duties of the Christian Ministry. A Pastoral Charge, addressed to Mr. George Sample, on his Ordination over the Baptist Church, assembling at West-Gate, Newcastle-upon-Tyne, October, 21, 1818.* London: Button and Son, 1819.

Stennett II, Joseph. *Sermon III. Preach'd at the Ordination of the Rev^d. Mr. David Rees, and two deacons; in a Church of Christ at Limehouse, Feb. 19, 1705–6* in *The Works Of the late Reverend and Learned Mr. Joseph Stennett.* London, 1731; II, 75–127.

Stennett, Samuel. *A Charge Delivered at the Ordination of the Rev. Mr. Caleb Evans* in *A Charge and Sermon, Together with an Introductory Discourse, and Confession of Faith, Delivered at the Ordination of the Rev. Mr. Caleb Evans, August 18, 1767, in Broad-Mead, Bristol.* Bristol: Broadmead Baptist Church, 1767; pages 38–71.

————. *A Sermon Preached at the Ordination of the Rev. Mr. Abraham Booth Feb.16, 1769, in Goodman's Fields* in *A Charge and Sermon together with an Introductory Discourse and Confession of Faith Delivered at the Ordination of the Rev. Mr. Abraham Booth Feb.16, 1769, in Goodman's Fields.* London: G. Keith/J. Buckland/W. Harris/B. Tomkins/J. Gurney, 1769; pages 53–90.

Tommas, John. *The duties incumbent on church members, and the manner in which they should be performed, represented and inforced* [*sic*] in *A Charge and Sermon, Together with an Introductory Discourse, and Confession of Faith, Delivered at the Ordination of the Rev. Mr. Caleb Evans, August 18, 1767, in Broad-Mead, Bristol.* Bristol: Broadmead Baptist Church, 1767; pages 74–99.

Turner, Daniel. *A Charge, etc.* in his and Caleb Evans, *A Charge and Sermon, Delivered at the Ordination of the Rev. Mr. Job David, October 7, 1773, at Frome, Somersetshire.* Bristol: W. Pine, T. Cadell, M. Ward, etc./London: J. Buckland, [1773]; pages 3–23.

Wallin, Benjamin. *The Obligations of a People to their faithful Minister. Represented in a Discourse Preached at the Ordination of the Revd. Mr. Samuel Burford, September 4, 1755.* London, 1755.

———. *A Charge Delivered at the Ordination of the Rev. Mr. Abraham Booth Feb.16, 1769, in Goodman's Fields* in *A Charge and Sermon together with an Introductory Discourse and Confession of Faith Delivered at the Ordination of the Rev. Mr. Abraham Booth Feb.16, 1769, in Goodman's Fields.* London: G. Keith/J. Buckland/W. Harris/B. Tomkins/J. Gurney, 1769; pages 28–51.